How to Help Your Child Succeed in School

Susan Stainback, EdD
and
William Stainback, EdD

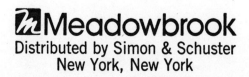
Distributed by Simon & Schuster
New York, New York

Library of Congress Cataloging-in-Publication Data

Stainback, Susan Bray.
   How to help your child succeed in school / Susan Stainback and William
Stainback.

   1. Home and school—United States. 2. Education—United States—Parent
participation. 3. Study, Method of 4. Academic achievement. I. Stainback,
William C. II. Title.
LC225.3.S73 1988 371.3'028'13—dc19 88-11952
ISBN 0-88166-117-1

Published by Meadowbrook Press, 18318 Minnetonka Boulevard, Deephaven, MN 55391

BOOK TRADE DISTRIBUTION by Simon & Schuster, a division of Simon &
Schuster, Inc., 1230 Avenue of the Americas, New York, NY 10020

S&S Ordering #: 0-671-67102-2

88 89 90 91 10 9 8 7 6 5 4 3 2 1

Printed in the United States of America

Acknowledgments

A number of people assisted us throughout the development and writing of this book. First, we would like to acknowledge the many parents and educators who read various rough drafts of the book and gave us valuable suggestions for improvement. They include: Henri Courtnage, J. W. Pollard, Bill and Georgie Bray, Marilyn Busch, Joyce Broell, Linda Gleissner, and George Stainback. We also owe Marilyn Busch special thanks for providing excellent typing assistance with an ever-pleasant, cheerful attitude. Finally, we would like to acknowledge our publisher, Bruce Lansky, and the staff at Meadowbrook for their guidance and assistance.

Contents

A Note to Parents... v

A Note to Teachers... vi

1. Introduction 1

2. Helping Your Child Organize for Study.............. 4

3. Promoting Good Study Skills................................. 10

4. Increasing Your Child's Motivation
   for Schoolwork 29

5. Managing School-Related Stress........................... 43

6. Overcoming Learning and
   Behavior Problems.. 59

7. Getting Involved in the Schools............................ 83

8. Finding Help When It Is Needed 90

9. Promoting Education in the Home....................... 95

   Appendix A (Parent's Form)................................. 105

   Appendix B (Teacher's Form)............................... 108

A Note to Parents

One of the most important concerns of parents today is their children's education. School success influences not only children's happiness and feelings of self-worth but also the quality of their adult lives.

Parents can help their children do better in school. In fact, parental help can affect school success as much as, or even more than, a child's IQ. According to national study groups, the difference between children who do poorly in school and those who do well often relates to what their parents do at home to help them.

So, what can you do to help your child? This book is designed to offer very specific and practical suggestions. We discuss how you can help your child to establish and maintain a study schedule, develop good study habits and skills, and, perhaps most important, become motivated to do schoolwork. We also describe how to help your child manage school-related stress and overcome learning and behavior problems. In addition, we provide information on communicating with school personnel, getting outside help when it's needed, and promoting a family environment that fosters educational success.

To help you clarify areas in which your child can improve his or her school performance, we have included a checklist (Appendix A) of habits and skills your child needs for school success. By completing the checklist, you can quickly identify what you can do at home to help. Appendix B contains a checklist for your child's teacher(s) to complete. It will provide additional information about what you can do at home, based on skills your child demonstrates in the classroom.

A good education is a gift you can give that will remain with your child throughout life. Unlike cars, stocks, or the dollar, it will never lose its value. We hope this book will help you to help your child get a good, quality education.

A Note to Teachers

With today's increasing emphasis on home and community involvement in education, a teacher's responsibility extends beyond the classroom. The growing level of parental interest means that teachers are gaining opportunities to develop partnerships with parents to foster children's educational growth. Parent-teacher conferences are standard practice, and, in many school systems, home visitations for teachers are becoming more common. Teachers need to know what parents can do at home to foster their children's educational success.

This book presents specific, practical ways parents can help their children attain and maintain school success. It provides you—as a concerned teacher—specific suggestions to give parents when their children are having difficulties that can be worked on at home. You might also want to recommend this book to parents who want to know how they can help their child at home or who have children with problems that we cover.

To help you determine the areas in which parents can help, we have included a checklist (Appendix B) of habits and skills all students need to develop at home. By completing this checklist and determining areas in which a student is either strong or in need of improvement, you can quickly give parents the information they need.

Neither the checklist nor the book is intended to cover specific curricular areas of study. Rather, our focus is on study habits and skills important to success in all subject areas—the habits and skills that parents can help their child to develop and practice.

Introduction

We live in an increasingly complex society in which getting a good eduction is no longer an option; it's a necessity. Education opens up career and social opportunities and increases any child's chance for leading a happy and productive life. Yet, many children don't do as well in school as they or their parents would like.

Fortunately, parents can help their children do better in school. Our purpose in this book is to show you the specific, practical ways you can help your children learn to do their best.

Can Your Child Be Helped?

All children can improve their school performance, from those who have a poor attitude toward schoolwork; to those who find it difficult to learn, understand, and remember information; to those who could excel with just a little extra motivation and a better understanding of study skills.

Children often show dramatic improvements in school performance when they learn how to overcome learning and behavior problems, respect education, and practice good study habits and skills.

How Is School Success Achieved?

School success doesn't just happen; it takes hard work. Children have to learn how to establish and maintain a study schedule, employ good study skills to learn efficiently and effectively, and be motivated to excel. The good news, however, is that these are all things you can foster in your child.

In addition to seeing that your child works hard, you must have high expectations. Parents in Japan and other Asian countries believe that with hard work and perseverance any child can master schoolwork, although some may master it more easily than others. As a consequence, Asian children's school achievement far exceeds that of their age-mates in many other countries, including the United States. Thus, to help your child succeed, you must guard against using learning problems or interests, or even your family's financial resources, as excuses for poor performance.

Why Do You Need to Help?

Children have a much better chance of doing their best in school when their parents become involved. In fact, national study groups have reported recently that parents play a critical role in their children's education.

Education should not be left solely to the schools. Parents have a responsibility to foster attitudes, values, habits, and skills that promote school success. As a nationally recognized education specialist noted, "Whether or not your child does well in school may, in large part, depend on you" (Claire Safran, *Reader's Digest,* September 1986).

When Should You Start Helping?

It's never too late or too early to start helping your child do better in school. Even students in high school or college can be helped to improve their school performance. And even preschool students can learn attitudes, habits, and skills that will build a solid foundation for success throughout their school years.

In short, you can help your child succeed in school, no matter what his or her age. The suggestions provided in this book apply to helping children whether they are in preschool, elementary school, or high school.

What Is the Best Way to Use This Book?

This book contains many ideas for helping children do better in school, but not all of the ideas are needed for every child. The checklist at the back of the book might help you determine your child's needs. We recommend that you trust your own judgment and use only those ideas you feel would be most helpful to your child.

We also recommend that you start by trying only a few of the suggestions in the book and gradually add to them after they are operating smoothly. Trying to do too much too fast could create an impossible job for both you and your child.

Conclusion

Excellence in education requires not only that schools offer quality programs and services, but that children do their best to learn and benefit from what the schools have to offer. As parents, you can be instrumental in helping your children do their best. After all, their education is far too important for you not to become involved.

Helping Your Child Organize for Study

Nothing is more important to effective studying than organization. Most of you have probably learned the value of organization for yourselves, and the suggestions in this chapter might seem quite obvious. Even so, you might want to scan the chapter to make sure that nothing in your child's situation has been overlooked.

The first key to organized studying is developing and maintaining a daily study schedule. The second is creating a quiet, comfortable place to study.

Scheduling Study Time

Planning the Study Schedule

Children who maintain a consistent, daily study schedule generally do well in school. It's best to talk with your child's teacher or teachers to determine how much study time to schedule, but you can use the following as a very rough guideline.

Ages 4 to 6: 15 to 30 minutes per day, 3 to 4 days per week

Ages 7 to 12: 1 to 2 hours per day, 5 days per week

Ages 13 to 18: 2 to 3 hours per day, 5 to 6 days per week

Making Yourself Available

Initially, schedule study time when you will be available to help. If you cannot help, you should find or hire someone who can. (How to hire good, but inexpensive, help for your child's study time is discussed in Chapter 8.)

Until your child develops the "study habit," you should help him with his study schedule and focus his attention on his schoolwork, when necessary. Telling your child periodically that you are pleased to see him working hard will help him maintain his study schedule.

Setting Aside the Same Time Each Day

If possible, schedule study time for the same time each day. (It's easier to remember to do something when we do it at the same time.) You might need to change the schedule periodically, but try to maintain consistency as much as possible.

A POINT TO PONDER

Several parents have told us that they find it helpful for the entire family to schedule a quiet hour or two each night. When they're not helping their children study, parents often use this time to pay bills; work on their taxes; read newpapers, magazines, or books; or make plans for the next day.

This is an excellent idea. Children are more inclined to study if everyone else in the house is working or doing something quietly, since it's difficult to study when others are laughing, talking, or watching TV. In addition, the children will see the parents as learners too.

Using All of the Scheduled Time

Don't permit your child to skip his scheduled study time or stop early on some days. For example, if the schedule calls for him to study from 4:30 to 6:00 P.M., Monday through Friday, it is important that he use all of that time to study.

If your child does not have anything to do or finishes early, he can read ahead or review previous work. You might want to ask his teacher(s) to provide a list of recommended readings or activities that he can do when no homework is assigned.

We realize that it might seem overly strict to require that your child stick to the schedule and do school-related work even when he has no assigned schoolwork. However, school success depends on your child *developing a habit* of studying consistently.

Developing "Time Plans"

In addition to helping organize a scheduled study time, you'll need to help your child learn to develop "time plans" for assignments. Students often receive homework assignments that are due not the next schoolday, but sometime later. Children often find these long-range assignments the most difficult, because they must break them down into manageable parts and set deadlines for completing each part so they can finish the entire task by the due date.

Too often, such assignments are left to the last possible day. When this happens, your child does not have adequate time to think about and work on the assignment and will turn out a less-than-adequate product.

When your child prepares a time plan, have him discuss it with you. Periodically check his plan to see if he is completing tasks on schedule. If he is not, find out why and help him figure out how to correct the problem. Time plans are crucial to your child's becoming a good student.

A POINT TO PONDER

According to recent studies, Asian-American children tend to do much better in school than many other children. After studying the situation, an economist at Stanford University explained that, "It is an old-fashioned story—if you work hard, you do well. Asian parents are teaching a lesson that otherwise isn't being taught in America anymore. Asian kids study harder than do white and black kids and are, therefore, getting better grades." The economist concluded, "Work works" (Sowell, *New York Times,* 3 August, 1986).

Making Study a Top Priority

If you and your child value school success, you must assign a top priority in your home to developing and maintaining a study schedule. If you permit a higher priority for other things (for example, watching certain television programs, playing sports, visiting with neighbors), you'll find it much more difficult to make time for scheduled study.

SUMMARY OF WAYS TO ESTABLISH A STUDY SCHEDULE

1. Help your child plan a study schedule.

2. Be available to work with your child during the scheduled study times.

3. Schedule the study sessions for the same time each day.

4. Help your child begin promptly and keep working for the entire scheduled time.

5. Encourage your child to make "time plans" for long-term assignments.

6. Make developing and maintaining the study schedule a top priority.

Arranging a Place to Study

A convenient and quiet place to study is a critical part of organized study—it makes studying much easier, more productive, and more pleasant. The following are guidelines for helping your child create his study area.

A Permanent Place to Work

Set aside a definite, permanent place to study. The room or area you and your child select should look and feel like a place to study and should contain only those items that suggest studying. Potential distractions such as a stereo, television, toys, hobbies, or magazines should be out of sight.

If at all possible, have your child use this area only for study and schoolwork. That way he will automatically be reminded of studying each time he enters it. Over time, going to the study area actually becomes a strong, unconscious reminder that it is study time, which makes getting started and sticking to the study schedule much easier.

Furnishings

Choose furniture for the study area that is comfortable and appropriate for your child's size. The height of the chair should allow your child's feet to rest firmly on the floor. The desk or table should be large enough to accommodate all the study tools that he will need.

STUDY AREA FOR A PRESCHOOL CHILD

Even preschool children need a study area, although it should be less formal than for older children.

The parents of a young preschool boy we know made a little study area in the corner of a room. It included a child-size table and chair and preschool materials and books. Although their son used the materials and books throughout the house at different times, the parents went with him to the study area for ten or fifteen minutes, three times a week, and helped him enjoy learning activities (for example, they read to him, or he counted to them). They made it both a family affair and fun time. In the process, they laid the foundation for their young son to develop the habits of having a study area and working at scheduled times on school-type activities.

Lighting

Your child needs to be as alert as possible during study time, and a well-lighted room increases alertness.

Good lighting also cuts down on glare. Glare is caused by focused lighting that produces sharp contrasts in brightness, with some areas of the study space well lighted and others dim or shadowed. Glare can tire eyes and also leads to slower and less accurate reading.

Pleasant, Attractive Surroundings

For most children, an attractive, pleasant study area can produce unconscious feelings of satisfaction and helps relax tensions that can interfere with mental work. A bleak, depressing study area can make your child unconsciously want to avoid the area.

Such seemingly trivial items in the study area as attractive pictures, curtains, a rug, and even flowers or a plant can improve a child's attitude toward schoolwork. By decorating the walls with certificates or diplomas your child or other family members have earned, or with pictures of a classroom, books, or people studying, you reinforce the study attitude.

SUMMARY OF WAYS TO DEVELOP A DESIRABLE STUDY AREA

1. Select a permanent study area.

2. Choose furniture that allows for solid support, fits your child's size, and provides adequate work space.

3. Make sure the area has bright, overhead, diffused light rather than sharp, direct light that casts shadows and causes glare.

4. Make the area a pleasant, attractive, desirable place to work.

Conclusion

Make sure that you arrange, evaluate, and plan both the study schedule and the place to study *with* your child. Your child needs to learn how to create a good work schedule and a study space so that he'll be able to continue his "study habit" throughout his life.

Promoting Good Study Skills

By developing practical study skills, your child can become a more effective learner. Good study skills can enhance any child's ability to learn more in less time and to understand and retain the information.

Study skills like those discussed in this chapter are most useful after a child has learned basic reading, writing, and arithmetic and has regular homework assignments—usually about the third grade. However, many parents encourage good study skills at home from the preschool years on. This early guidance can give the child a solid foundation for learning and using the study skills.

Studying for Understanding

When children understand what they study, they remember it more easily than if they simply memorize it. More importantly, when children understand what they learn, they use it to solve problems or answer questions in classroom discussions or on tests.

You can help your child study for understanding.

Tackling Difficult Material First

Teach your child to begin each study session with the most difficult assignments—a fresh mind understands difficult material more easily. Have her do easier tasks and review later in the study session, since they don't require such intense concentration.

A POINT TO PONDER

If your child is having trouble with a homework assignment, don't start out by trying to give her an in-depth explanation. First, ask her to explain what she does understand so you can tell what aspect she's finding difficult. You must understand what she already knows before you can help effectively. If you try to help too quickly, you might actually confuse rather than help her.

Using a Survey-Read-Resurvey Approach

When your child studies a chapter in a school text or a reference book, encourage her to use the "survey-read-resurvey" method. This method makes information easier to understand than simply reading from beginning to end.

Have your child first survey the chapter for the main ideas, perhaps by reading the introduction and summary to the chapter. It's also helpful to look at the title of the chapter, the topic and subtopic headings, pictures, maps, graphs, and any study questions at the beginning or end.

Once your child understands the main ideas, she should read the chapter carefully. Encourage her to underline, highlight, or take notes on the main ideas and important details while she reads.

Finally, have her look back through, or resurvey, the chapter by rereading the introduction and summary and closely examining the title, the information under each of the headings, and the information in the pictures.

You can introduce the survey-read-resurvey method to very young children when you look at pictures with them or read them a story. Survey the picture or story in a general way, then look at or read the specifics, and then resurvey in a general way. This approach can lead your child into developing the habit of using the survey-read-resurvey method.

Encouraging Development of a Viewpoint

To increase their understanding, children need to think about what they are studying and develop a "point of view." For example, when your child is studying weather in science class, you could encourage her to form an opinion about what causes rain.

Once your child has a point of view, she can then figure out what information supports or does not support it. This approach forces her to think and understand rather than passively accept or memorize facts. Encourage your child to be ready to modify her point of view as she gathers information.

Promoting a Questioning Approach

When your child is either beginning a new area of study or delving deeper into a topic, encourage her to formulate questions both before and during surveying, reading, and resurveying.

Have her make up questions to which she does not know the answers. Her task then becomes one of finding the answers. Role playing and games often develop from such questioning. For instance, if you were George Washington at Valley Forge, what would you do? Your child can then read and find out what George Washington did. Even in the early years of reading to your child, you can encourage her to ask questions.

Once your child learns how to question and think, studying becomes more interesting, more fun, and more meaningful. Note that it is not critical *which* questions your child asks. Asking questions of any kind will promote an active, involved, and thoughtful approach to studying.

A POINT TO PONDER

Children learn to think, reason, and understand more readily if parents maintain a home environment that encourages them to:

1. Think of solutions to their own everyday problems, and think about the advantages and disadvantages of each solution.

2. Ask questions about the world around them.

3. Provide evidence and reasons for their opinions.

Encouraging Summarization

Another way to help children study is to encourage them to summarize. There are a number of effective ways to summarize. Using one or more of them can help children improve their understanding, since they must look for and note important points in the material. Also, preparing summaries enables children to review quickly and effectively before tests or exams.

(1) *Outlining* is one way to summarize. The simplest way to outline is to use the textbook headings and subheadings, listing the major points covered underneath each heading.

(2) *Note taking* is another summarizing technique that fosters understanding and memorization. To take notes, your child simply writes down or tape records in her own words the facts and ideas she considers most critical. The benefit of note taking is that your child not only summarizes what she studies, but also translates it into her own words. She summarizes in a way she can understand, which will help her in later review.

(3) *Underlining or highlighting* important key ideas, facts, and details also helps in study and review. Generally, it's best if your child marks only critical phrases or terms that remind her of important points. If she underlines or highlights most of the material, it will be of little use in a quick review. Before she marks any words or phrases, she should read a complete section or block of material to determine the most important points.

Encouraging an Organized Approach to Study

Encourage your child to organize important facts and information into categories whenever possible. For example, when she studies history, she might organize the information into important ideas, events, people, and dates. Or, when studying math, she might organize it into formulas to remember, principles to follow, definitions to understand, and types of problems to solve. The mere process of putting things into categories can help her recognize, understand, and remember essential information.

Fostering Reflection

When your child is studying an assignment, she should take a few minutes at regular intervals to try to recall what she just learned. When she does this, she might want to talk to herself about it or write it down.

If your child understands what she just studied, she will be able to visualize it and talk to herself intelligently about it. If she cannot, encourage your child to reread or restudy the material until she can.

During reflection time, most children will realize what they have not learned or cannot recall. They often then look back through the assignment until they can remember it.

Using a Different Textbook

If your child has trouble understanding the information in one of her textbooks, you might want to find other textbooks that cover the same topic. Textbooks explain things in different ways, and some explanations are clearer than others. Merely reading a different explanation sometimes helps a child understand something better.

Teach your child to be selective when using these resource textbooks. For instance, if she is having trouble understanding a certain principle in physics, encourage her to find that specific information in the resource texts. Too often, a child begins studying material without evaluating its intended purpose. Help her save time by showing her how to use the table of contents and index to find what she needs. This approach helps focus her attention on what she needs to learn.

Using a Combination of Study Experiences

Finally, a child has a better chance of learning and understanding if she can experience what she studies in a combination of ways—by seeing it, hearing it, saying it, and writing it down. Thus, encourage her to read the material, write about it, listen to it on a tape recorder, and talk about it either to herself or to you.

ENCOURAGING STUDYING FOR UNDERSTANDING

1. Encourage your child to study the most difficult assignments first and save the easiest for last.

2. Explain the survey-read-resurvey method.

3. Encourage your child to develop a point of view when studying.

---

4. Show her how to ask and answer questions when she studies.

5. Encourage her to take notes or otherwise summarize what she studies.

6. Have her look up explanations in other textbooks when she has difficulty.

7. Encourage her to organize the information she studies into categories.

8. Tell her to take a few minutes at regular intervals while studying to try to recall what she has just learned.

9. Encourage her to experience what she studies in a combination of ways—by seeing it, hearing it, writing it down, and saying it.

To a large extent, success in school depends upon learning how to study for understanding. A number of additional suggestions for helping children understand what they study can be found in Chapter 6 under the heading "Difficulty in Understanding."

Studying for Tests

If your child studies regularly and uses her study skills to understand the information, she should be well prepared for tests. However, you can suggest additional steps that will improve her performance on tests.

Clarifying the Content

Focus your child's attention on finding out and reviewing the specific material to be covered on an upcoming test. Encourage her to listen closely when the teacher discusses what the test will cover. Also encourage her to ask the teacher questions about the test content if it isn't clear.

If your child has an upcoming test on the American Revolution, for example, she might need to clarify things such as: Will the test cover just battles and dates, or will it also include reasons for these events and how the events have shaped American lives? What specific textbook chapters will it cover? Will the test include material in the class notes?

If your child still finds it difficult to understand what will be covered on tests, you may want to contact her teacher for suggestions.

Learning from Previous Tests

Encourage your child to briefly review previous tests when studying for an upcoming test. This review will remind her of how the teacher asks questions and what kind of information needs to be recalled. Your child then will be less likely to prepare for the test in the wrong way or concentrate on unimportant information.

Finding Out the Type of Test

You might want to discuss with your child what type of test questions or problems the test will include and how she might best prepare for them. If the teacher does not mention what type of test it will be, encourage your child to ask.

A child who knows what type of test questions will be included—essay or discussion questions, or objective questions such as true or false, multiple choice, or fill-in-the-blank—has a much better chance of doing well. In general, when studying for objective questions, your child should concentrate on details and specific information. For essay or discussion questions, she should get a wide background on the subject and then try to list the important ideas and themes.

Making Up Practice Test Questions

Your child can better her chances for successful test taking by preparing and answering practice questions. For example, if the test will require making up sentences using vocabulary words, have her practice making sentences using the words likely to be covered. Similarly, if the test will require her to solve certain types of algebra problems, have her make up and solve practice problems.

Encourage and help your child, at first, to develop practice questions. She can even put them together into a test to practice taking at home. She can score the test by checking the answers against the studied material. This approach can make tests less threatening and more familiar to your child while providing a review of the material.

Some children find it helpful to write questions on the fronts of index or note cards and answers on the backs. By doing this, your child can read a question to herself, try to answer it from recall, and then quickly check to see whether the answer is correct. Or, your child can play a game similar to "Trivial Pursuit" with you, a sibling, or someone else. This can be an enjoyable, fun, and effective way to study for tests.

STUDYING FOR A TEST WITH A FRIEND

Children sometimes want to study for a test with a friend. The two of them can take turns explaining difficult material to each other, making up questions, and asking each other the questions.

Many children profit from studying together. They must, however, be serious about studying. If they use study time for other things (such as discussing boyfriends or girlfriends), they would be better off not studying together.

Reviewing

Your child's test performance will probably improve if she briefly reviews materials she has already studied. She should review during each study period, not just before a test.

The time when children are most likely to forget information is right after they first learn it. Developing the habit of periodically reviewing study materials can help your child eliminate the problem of immediate forgetting.

Reviewing does not take long if your child does it regularly and uses the outlines or notes she made when she was first learning the material (as discussed in the previous section on Studying for Understanding). She should refer to the original material only when a point in her notes or outline is unclear.

Helping your child develop the habit of consistent review will not only improve her understanding and memory, it will also eliminate the need for last-minute "cramming." Also, she will be better prepared for class discussions and unannounced quizzes or tests.

Memorizing

Teach your child to wait to memorize information until shortly before a test, since the things we memorize we tend to forget soon (unless we use the information frequently, such as a friend's telephone number).

One of the best ways for your child to memorize something is to use all of her senses, that is, to look at it closely, say it, hear it, write it down, and repeat all of these steps several times.

Although memorization without understanding is not the best way to learn, there are times when rote memorization is necessary—for example, in learning definitions in math, formulas in physics, and dates in history.

Hints for Taking Tests

The night before a test, spend a few minutes with your child going over how to take tests. The following hints will help her when she is facing any type of exam. Tell her to:

(1) Take a few minutes to relax just before the test. Excessive anxiety decreases her chances of doing her best. To relax, she might try sitting back, breathing deeply, relaxing her muscles, and thinking about being in a quiet, pleasant setting. The relaxation exercises discussed in Chapter 5 ("How Can You Help Your Child Cope with Stress?") might help. A relaxed, refreshed student can concentrate better on any task.

(2) Quickly survey the whole test when it is handed out. This will help her estimate how much time to spend on each question or section of the test.

(3) Pay close attention to the test directions. Answering a test the way the teacher wants usually adds points to the score.

(4) First answer the questions or parts she knows best. Children often spend too much time on a part of a test they know little about and then have too little time to answer what they do know.

(5) Concentrate on one question at a time and read it carefully before answering. Many children read a test too quickly and make careless mistakes. It's difficult to give the correct answer if you don't fully understand the question.

(6) Put a check mark in front of any question she is uncertain about and go on to the next question. If she spends too much time on a difficult question, she might get frustrated, which will interfere with her ability to answer other questions. (Instead, she can go back to the difficult question after she completes the rest of the test.)

(7) Try to rewrite difficult questions in her own words. This approach helps her clarify what information she needs and remember what she learned about the topic.

(8) Look carefully for any qualifying words such as *usually, always, most, never,* or *some* when answering true/false questions. These words often provide the key as to whether the question is true or false.

(9) Take a few minutes to list or outline the major points she wants to make before she answers an essay question. Students who take a few minutes to organize their ideas before they write usually answer essay questions much better. She might also try simply restating the question as the first part of her answer. This technique can help her make sure that she really answers the question.

(10) Always check over or review answers before turning in a test. This is one of the most important things to do. Careless mistakes causing incorrect answers can often be easily corrected. On essay tests, it is usually a good idea to refine and add, if necessary, to the original answer. However, you should caution your child not to change an answer too quickly if she is not sure it is wrong. This is particularly true for objective-type tests. When in doubt, the first answer is often the correct one.

(11) Be as neat as possible. Although many children do not believe that neatness counts, with most teachers it does.

Preparing Young Children for Future Test Taking

Young children enjoy pop quizzes or question games about something they have just learned. The quiz might consist of only a couple of questions. As a reward for getting correct answers, your child might earn a special treat, such as a favorite food for dinner or a trip to the ice cream shop. In this way, she can get familiar with tests at an early age, develop a positive attitude toward taking them, and look upon them as a challenge.

HINTS ON STUDYING FOR TESTS

1. Discuss with your child the importance of finding out specifically what will be covered on an upcoming test and what type of test questions there will be.

2. Encourage her to briefly review any previous tests.

3. Help her make up and answer practice questions.

4. Explain the importance of reviewing regularly rather than only right before a test.

5. Encourage your child to save memorization until shortly before the test.

6. Give your child hints on how to take tests.

Finding and Using Resource Materials

The basic resource materials your child uses for homework assignments are the textbooks, workbooks, and papers that her teacher provides. However, these materials might not always be enough. Sometimes your child will need to find out more about a topic than the teacher and textbook provide. This extra information may include anything from pictures of barnyard animals, to descriptions or comparisons of political parties, to clearer explanations of how to work a set of math problems.

A child who knows how to find and use resource materials has a better chance of succeeding in school. You can help her learn how.

Additional Textbooks

If your child finds it difficult to understand the information in one of her textbooks, it often helps, as noted earlier, to get other textbooks on the same topic. These extra books need not be expensive. Often, you can borrow or buy used books from the school or buy secondhand books at garage sales, from older children in the neighborhood, or at consignment stores or used bookstores. Collecting a variety of such books costs little, yet may benefit your child considerably.

Study Aids

You can buy other helpful study aids in most bookstores. One popular type is a brief summary of novels and other classic books that are frequently assigned as homework reading (for example, *Cliffs Notes*). Your child should always read the entire book, but *Cliffs Notes* can provide very useful summaries for reviewing before a test, writing a book report, or clarifying a chapter, passage, or point.

Other study aids provide examples and practice exercises for various standardized tests. Although your child needs in-depth knowledge of the material to be covered, these test booklets can help her prepare for the types of questions she might encounter.

Also available are study aids such as cassette tapes for learning foreign languages and books that simplify English, history, algebra, geometry, calculus, physics, chemistry, and many other subjects. You and your child might want to visit several major bookstores to become familiar with the range of study aids available.

Encyclopedias

Guide your child in the habit of using encyclopedias. Encyclopedias summarize current knowledge on a wide range of subjects, with each summary usually written by a leading authority on the subject. Encyclopedias provide a good orientation to any subject your child is studying.

A set of encyclopedias is well worth the investment. Even if you can't afford to buy a set, you'll find that most school and public libraries have several sets that cater to students of all ages.

Dictionaries

A dictionary appropriate for your child's level of understanding is a valuable resource. You can help your child's chances for school success not only by making sure she has a dictionary in her study area, but also by encouraging her to use it whenever she encounters an unfamiliar word. Encouraging her to pay attention to new words and get into the "dictionary habit" can help her better understand explanations or readings, become a faster, more accurate reader, and a better communicator.

Note, however, that although it is important for children to use the dictionary, you must be careful to encourage them to use it only when they actually need to. If your child uses the dictionary too much when she is studying, she risks missing the meaning of what she studies by constantly switching her attention to something else.

Also, if you tell your child to look up a word in the dictionary, give her some clues, such as the first few letters. If she gets no help finding difficult words, she might become frustrated and, as a result, reluctant to use reference books.

Libraries

Even if your child's study area has plenty of resource materials, you'll sometimes need to find additional ones. The best places to check are the school library, the public library, or a local college library.

The first few times your child goes to a library, she might not know how to use the library effectively or where to find the books or materials she needs. Help her arrange an appointment with someone who can explain how to find different materials. Most libraries have staff members who are happy to do this.

EARLY LIBRARY EXPOSURE

You can get your child acclimated to the library at a very early age. Most public libraries have Saturday morning film or story-telling programs for preschool and primary school children. By attending such activities, your child can develop a positive attitude toward the library and the people in it.

If possible, provide your child with money and instructions to photocopy material that she needs from any books or articles she can't check out. Most libraries have photocopy machines. Copying material by hand can waste hours of time that your child could better use studying, completing a school project, or writing a paper. Encourage her to write down the source for any material she copies in case she needs this information later.

Note that copyright laws dictate how much you can copy from any single source. Your child should ask the librarian for advice.

FINDING AND USING RESOURCE MATERIALS

1. Help your child get supplementary textbooks that give different views or presentations of the material in her assigned books.

2. Help her gather and use any published study aids that summarize or explain information she is studying or provide practice exercises.

3. Show her how to use encyclopedias and dictionaries.

4. Help her learn to use school and community libraries.

5. Provide her with money for photocopying at the library, so she doesn't have to copy by hand all the information she needs.

Writing Papers

In general, teachers give explanations and directions for writing papers. Nevertheless, many children find it very difficult to do. Parents can help them make the task easier.

Selecting a Topic

Unless the teacher assigns a specific topic, the first task is to select one. You can help your child select a topic by encouraging your child to:

(1) Consider a topic from her daily life or family experiences. (For example, if a family of bluebirds lives in your yard, a good science paper topic might be, "How Baby Bluebirds Learn to Fly.")

(2) Look for topic ideas in the tables of contents or the major headings of textbooks.

(3) Look for ideas by skimming encyclopedias and other reference books.

When your child is choosing a topic, encourage her to focus on something from her daily life that interests her. This increases the chances that she will stick with the project and complete it.

USING FAMILY MEMBERS AS RESOURCES

Our nephew was having considerable difficulty settling on a topic for a science paper. He was not interested in science and didn't want to begin his project. But one day, while watching his dad at work, the two of them began discussing how a heat pump works.

Building on this interest, our nephew decided to do his science project on heat pumps. He used his dad and other members of his dad's heating and air conditioning business as resources. Not only did he get an "A" on his paper, his teacher also sent his parents a note telling them that he was thoroughly knowledgeable and confident in presenting the project to his class. In fact, his presentation was so interesting and informative that his classmates started a lively discussion on heat pumps.

Make sure your child doesn't choose a topic that is too broad to cover in one paper. Unfortunately, without guidance many children tend to select a broad topic such as "Presidents of the United States," rather than a more specific topic such as "President Abraham Lincoln." Too broad a topic not only makes the paper difficult to complete but also makes your child feel overwhelmed and frustrated when collecting the background information.

Gathering Background Information

It doesn't matter if the paper is historical, scientific, creative, problem-solving, or fictional, the best first step is usually to gather background information before beginning to write.

Help your child find novel and interesting sources of background material. For example, in addition to school textbooks and reference books from home or the library, your child might look for maps, pictures, or displays in historical, science, or art museums. Help her find people in the community who are experts on the topic, and whom she could interview. Many people would enjoy an opportunity to share their knowledge and experiences. Also, if the paper is on something that your child can observe, such as "How Cheese Is Made," she might want to visit a cheese factory to see the process and talk with the workers and managers.

Be sure to tell her to take notes on whatever she sees, hears, or reads when she is gathering background information.

Organizing the Paper

Once your child selects a topic and collects background information, she needs to determine how to organize the paper. You can make several suggestions to assist with this task.

(1) Encourage your child to review the topic and the materials she has collected and then write down the purpose or theme of the paper. Writing a few sentences stating what the paper will be about can help her clarify and narrow the topic. It also will provide both a beginning for the paper and a sense of confidence about completing it.

(2) After your child has clarified the purpose of the paper, encourage her to consider what subtopics she plans to cover, as well as the important points and details under each subtopic. This plan provides the basis for a written outline. It can also help her determine whether there is any missing information she needs to collect.

By preparing an outline, your child can see how she can organize the whole paper. Preparing an outline also breaks down the writing task into manageable parts so your child doesn't get confused or overwhelmed by all the information she has collected.

(3) You might want to suggest that your child look at how successful writers have organized papers on her subject. She can use a good model to guide the organization and development of her own paper. For example, she can examine how good writers introduce their topic, arrange the core of the paper, and conclude or summarize it. She can also see how they begin and end their paragraphs and sections. However, make sure your child develops her own sentences and ideas and does not rely too heavily on the model for content, sentence structure, or wording.

Getting Started

When your child has collected and organized all the information, she can begin writing. She can use her existing outline to develop the paper part by part.

You can help her in these ways:

(1) Encourage your child to write down what she wants to say without worrying too much about grammar, spelling, punctua-

tion, or capitalization. Once she writes down the basic content, she can go back and correct any mistakes.

(2) Encourage her to use simple sentences and words. In general, short sentences made up of common words from everyday life (and from the field of study she is writing about) make a paper clear, direct, and understandable. One of the most common mistakes is assuming that long, complex sentences with uncommon words improve the quality of a paper. Instead, they usually make it hard to read and understand.

A POINT TO PONDER

Don't wait to encourage your child to write until she is assigned her first school paper. Even preschool and first-grade children can learn to scribble and write. Let your child write anything she wants to—such as a letter to a friend or a description of a day at grandma's house.

By encouraging and reinforcing your child's early attempts at writing, you can help lay a solid foundation for formal school writing. Even if your child's writing just looks like scribbles and squiggles or makes little sense, encourage her to continue. Ask her what the writing means and then help her formulate a few of the letters better or spell a few of the words.

Don't be critical of mistakes in forming letters, spellings, punctuation, capitalization, or the other mechanics of writing. As your child writes more and more, she will gradually learn these things with help from you and her teachers. The important thing is that she continue writing no matter how crude her beginning attempts happen to be.

Children who don't write until they learn good handwriting, spelling, sentence structure, and punctuation seldom learn to be good writers. In short, children learn to be good writers primarily by writing. They gradually learn the amenities *while* writing, not before writing.

Polishing the Paper

Once your child writes the paper, encourage her to "polish" it before she shows it to anyone else. That is, she should review each sentence, paragraph, and section for how the ideas fit together and for spelling, grammar, neatness, and clarity. Concentrating on content and communicating ideas might be her first concern when she is writing, but she must also address these other concerns before the paper is finished.

Sharing with Others

Finally, encourage your child to share her polished paper with you and anyone else willing to read it and suggest improvements. Sharing it might bring her useful suggestions for making it easier to understand and for catching important omissions, breaks in logic, errors, or misinterpretation of facts. Comments from readers give your child the opportunity to refine the paper before she turns it in to her teacher.

WRITING PAPERS

Encourage your child to:

1. Select a topic.

2. Gather background information.

3. Outline and organize the content.

4. Write the paper.

5. Polish the paper.

6. Share the paper with others for suggested improvements.

Conclusion

By developing good study skills, your child can learn and complete school assignments much better. Good study skills can actually help teach her to learn efficiently and effectively.

Be very careful, however, about your role in this process. You can help your child learn good study skills by providing tips on how to study, encouraging her to use them, and providing resources such as time, tools, and support. However, take care that *you* don't do any of her homework. *Your child* must do each assignment herself to benefit from it.

Increasing Your Child's Motivation for Schoolwork

The setting, schedule, habits, and skills your child uses to learn can greatly affect his success in school. However, one key element must be present for him to become a successful learner: motivation. No child can be successful in school unless he has the desire to learn and succeed. In addition, as your child grows older and finds himself facing more and more study situations without your support and direction, his inner motivation direction becomes critical.

You can help your child increase his motivation and self-direction.

Setting Daily Study Goals

Most people recognize that study goals can help a child be more organized and focused during study sessions. What many people don't know is that establishing and completing daily study goals also increase motivation. Realistic, daily study goals provide something to strive for that is both clear and immediately attainable. Also, the more often a child feels a sense of accomplishment in completing schoolwork-related goals, the more motivated he is likely to become for doing schoolwork. Thus, establishing realistic, daily study goals is important. In fact, in our opinion, nothing is more critical in motivating your child for schoolwork.

When helping your child develop daily study goals, you'll need to keep the following in mind.

Deriving Goals from Homework Assignments

Help your child develop goals based either on new homework assignments or on reviewing and practicing old assignments. Examples of goals might be:

- Complete the ten assigned math problems and check the answers with dad.

- Read five pages of chapter three in my social studies book and then make up and answer two questions per page. Check my answers against the text.

- Decide on the topic for a short story I'm going to write for Mrs. Jones' class.

- Practice spelling eight words from my personal notebook of hard-to-spell words.

The goals must be achievable. Four or five small goals—which your child can reach one by one—work better than one larger goal. The goals also should be specific and clear. To feel a sense of accomplishment and increased motivation, your child must be able to recognize when he has accomplished a goal.

Listing the Goals

Have your child list the goals for each study session on a sheet of paper. Listing them should not take more than a few minutes. Having the list for ready reference during study time will remind your child frequently of what he needs to do.

Checking Off Goals as They Are Completed

Encourage your child to check off each goal as he finishes it. The check marks will give him a sense of accomplishment, which in turn will provide an incentive to keep going.

When his scheduled study time is over and all his goals are checked off, let your child do something he enjoys (for example, watching a television show or having a favorite snack). Help him associate something very pleasant and positive with completing his study time and goals.

Formulating Long-Term Goals

Establishing short-term daily goals is essential for motivation, but formulating long-term goals can also help, especially with older children. A long-term goal might be the chance to pursue a particular career or acceptance at a respected university.

You might want to help your child formulate a long-term goal and envision how it will feel when he accomplishes it. Just take a few minutes periodically to daydream with your child about his future. Such daydreaming often helps inspire a child and motivates him to study hard.

SETTING GOALS

1. Encourage your child to set daily goals for schoolwork.

2. Show him how to establish clear, specific, and achievable goals.

3. Be sure he keeps the list of goals on his desk.

4. Have him check off each goal when he completes it.

5. Help him envision long-term goals.

Establishing goals is not difficult. You can help your child learn to do it very quickly, and he will benefit throughout his school years and adult life.

Many, if not most, well-organized adults set up a brief list of goals they want to accomplish each day. Goals provide clear direction and, when completed, a sense of satisfaction that in turn leads to increased motivation.

Recognizing Achievements

All of us want to be recognized for our hard work and achievements. This is as true for children as it is for adults.

Children tend to gravitate toward and enjoy things that bring them recognition. As a result, one of the best ways to motivate a child for schoolwork is to reward his school-related achievements.

Catching Your Child Achieving

Focus on what your child does right, that is, look for achievements. Try to actually "catch" your child completing study goals or any other aspect of schoolwork.

In their book, *Write From the Start*, Donald Graves and Virginia Stuart provide an excellent example of parents focusing on a young girl's achievements.

One day, a four-and-a-half-year-old named Emily called to her parents, "Look. I made a word! I spelled SIR with my blocks." Her parents looked down and saw S-G-H-Y-R. They realized that they had an important decision to make, because their reaction could influence her future attempts. Emily had shown that she understood the purpose of the written word. She knew that words have meaning, letters make words, and at least some of those letters correspond with sounds. She wanted to write and had taken the risk of trying it on her own. Her parents had two choices. They could point out all that she knew—how to place letters from left to right and how to sound out the first and last letters—or they could say, "That's not how you spell *sir*." In short, they could either encourage her to keep trying or convince her, and themselves, that she wasn't ready to write.

Recognizing that this occasion was another first, like Emily's first tooth, first spoken word, and first step, the parents chose to congratulate her. "Look how well you did at sounding out these letters all by yourself," they said. "You heard the *s* and the *r* sounds."

In this example, the parents recognized and praised their daughter's very important achievement. Instead, they could have ignored it or focused on what she had done wrong. But they realized that if they focused on Emily's achievement, she would be more eager to continue trying to improve.

A POINT TO PONDER

A key to improving children's school success is to make them feel successful. Train yourself to look for the good things your child does—to look for success. Let your child know you like it and encourage it. Success breeds confidence and further success, so if you focus on, expect, and recognize success, your child will be more successful.

In recognizing your child's achievements, however, be careful to focus on accomplishments that are new or challenging. Too much recognition for every achievement, no matter how trivial, might make your recognition lose its value.

Also, be sure to make clear which accomplishments you are recognizing. If you don't, your child might associate your recognition with a mistake, leading to incorrect learning. In Emily's case, for example, the parents praised their daughter for trying to sound out letters and getting the first and last ones correct, not for correct spelling.

Rewarding Achievements

For most children, recognition and praise from their parents are very pleasant rewards for hard work. However, you might also want to provide more concrete rewards for achievements. Providing rewards for doing schoolwork is *not* bribery. Bribery is payment for something illegal or illicit, and doing schoolwork is neither.

After your child has successfully completed something, such as scheduled study time, or a study goal, let him do something else he really enjoys—for example, playing a game or calling a friend. If you do this often enough, it will help to motivate him to do homework.

Choose rewards that are a natural part of your environment, rather than something contrived or uncommon—especially if you want rewards for good study habits to become an ongoing part of your child's daily routine. However, when your child really works hard to achieve a specific goal (for example, good grades on a report card), you might want to do something really special to celebrate, like go to an amusement park or a movie.

As Claire Safran, an education specialist, recently pointed out, "Achievement may be its own reward, but special privileges are a spur. If you take your youngster out for pizza after an athletic achievement, for example, why not after an academic achievement?" (Claire Safran, *Reader's Digest*, September 1985).

DESSERT TIME

A friend told us that in his home, the family schedules quiet homework time for after dinner. They serve dessert as a reward only after the children finish their homework.

Here are some points to keep in mind when rewarding school achievements:

(1) Never provide a reward *before* an achievement, but do provide it as soon *after* the achievement as possible. If you must wait a while, tell your child that the reward is coming and then remind him what it's for when you give it to him.

(2) In the beginning, reward small steps or achievements. For example, reward your child for completing each session's study goals as opposed to rewarding him only for good grades on a report card. You must get your child "hooked" on success and recognition. After he starts getting good grades, you can gradually start requiring greater achievements for earning rewards.

(3) Be sure that the rewards you give your child are actually reinforcing him. A reward must be something he really cares about or it won't help motivate him.

(4) Finally, you must *not* provide any rewards when your child doesn't study or complete his study goals. However, don't let this situation occur too often—you want to avoid failure if at all possible. Schedule study times and set goals that are reasonable and clearly within your child's ability. If you know your child has done his best and failed, you'll need to help him to make his study schedules and goals more realistic.

Remember that success breeds success and failure breeds failure. Be sure to help your child create a situation where he can succeed if he puts forth the effort.

In general, young children approach schoolwork with curiosity and a desire to learn. By recognizing, encouraging, and rewarding achievements, both parents and teachers can help children maintain and enhance this desire to learn. As children continue to learn and achieve, their increasing knowledge becomes a reward in itself.

RECOGNIZING YOUR CHILD'S ACHIEVEMENTS

1. Focus on what your child does right.

2. Be sure that rewards follow studying and school achievements.

---

3. In general, use rewards that are a natural part of your home life.

4. Don't provide any rewards when your child doesn't study or complete his study goals.

What to Do if Your Child Breaks Study Rules

Children can be motivated to study hard and succeed in school if their parents provide clear goals and reward achievements, but they can also be motivated by the knowledge of what will happen if they don't study hard and do well. That is, your child must understand what will happen if he does not do what is required. If he breaks study rules or does his work poorly, inaccurately, or not at all, he must understand the unpleasant consequences that will result.

Stating Consequences in Advance

You and your child should decide ahead of time what the consequences will be for breaking study rules or not doing homework. That way, your child understands what will happen if he chooses to break a rule or not study. Also, by having him help determine the consequences, he will be more likely to see them as fair. Examples of serious unpleasant consequences are losing opportunities to play with friends, watch a favorite television program, or go on a planned trip to the zoo.

Note that you might sometimes need to use minor unpleasant consequences that you haven't planned ahead of time. Such a mild consequence might be frowning when your child chats on the phone to a friend during study time, or commenting "This will need to be redone" when you're looking over a messy or incorrect homework assignment. However, be sure to tell your child clearly what is acceptable. For these two examples, you might say "You can talk to your friend after you finish your homework" or "You'll need to copy this paper over more neatly so your teacher can read it." In this way, you can teach your child what are acceptable and unacceptable study habits.

Using Unpleasant Consequences Sparingly

Don't use too many unpleasant consequences. You want your child to become a successful, happy, confident learner. Using negative consequences too frequently could cause the opposite result—he could lose both his confidence and his desire to learn.

As a very rough rule of thumb, your child should receive rewards over ninety percent, and perhaps up to one hundred percent, of the time. If you are using negative consequences more than ten percent of the time, reevaluate what you are doing. You might want to talk with the teacher or change your rules and standards to make sure they are challenging, yet within your child's ability.

Choosing Consequences Carefully

When you use unpleasant consequences, be sure they are meaningful enough that your child will want to avoid them. However, make sure they are not so costly to your child that he gives up hope. For example, if you ground your child for one weekend, it's a serious, meaningful consequence that he will want to avoid. However, because it's a reasonable consequence, he won't give up all hope for his future social life.

If, on the other hand, you ground him for a month, he might feel that he'll never be able to resume his normal weekend social life. To many children, a month is forever! If your child gives up hope, he might see little need to work the next week ("I am grounded forever anyway!").

Be sure to keep in mind your child's age, personality, and interests when you're considering how severe a consequence should be.

Avoiding a Negative Atmosphere

Finally, make sure you find and eliminate any negative feelings toward school or studying. For example, don't nag or complain about your child's performance. Often, parents do this with good intentions—to encourage their children to do better. However, a child can develop such negative feelings about schoolwork that he learns to dislike it and tries to avoid it or withdraw from it. This avoidance often shows up as daydreaming or getting distracted easily. He might be there physically, but his mind might well be on something else.

Make sure you plan your approach to breaking rules ahead of time, and you should involve your child in the decisions. Also, make sure that you help create a positive atmosphere surrounding schoolwork, avoiding negative consequences if possible.

If you do need to use unpleasant consequences, make sure you recognize your child's next efforts. Don't hesitate to let him know when he does a good job, even if it's only in one subject area or on one accomplishment. In fact, look for school achievements—try to "catch" him studying hard and doing well.

You want to help your child be a happy, confident, responsible learner. A negative atmosphere can hurt your efforts to do this.

DEALING WITH UNDESIRABLE BEHAVIOR

1. Be sure that you and your child determine ahead of time what the consequences will be for breaking study rules or not doing schoolwork.

2. Use as few negative consequences as possible.

3. Make sure that negative consequences are meaningful and sufficiently unpleasant to discourage rule breaking.

4. Be careful to avoid a negative atmosphere surrounding school and studying activities.

Instilling Respect for Education

To motivate your child, you must go beyond helping him set study goals, rewarding achievements, and punishing rule breaking. You must also instill in him a respect for education. Children's attitudes toward education are predominantly influenced by their parents' guidance and examples. Thus, you have a major responsibility to help your child develop a healthy respect for education. Unless he learns this respect, none of the other motivational techniques will be of real or lasting value.

Showing Respect

Always demonstrate respect for education. Show pride in any new information you learn, and be eager to share the information with your child. Also, show respect whenever a neighbor, friend, or relative gets a good education. Never belittle the value of learning, even in jest, in front of your child. Unfortunately, we have seen parents make remarks in front of their child such as, "School taught me little that helps me in my work." Such statements clearly tell a child that, from his parents' point of view, education is of little practical value. Be sure you don't make this mistake. Instead, show your respect for education in everything you say and do.

Talking About School Activities

Ask your child, with genuine interest, about his classes. Take time to listen to and discuss any choices he is making about school activities, programs, or courses. Simply by talking with your child about school you'll communicate your belief in the importance of education.

DON'T GIVE UP

If you ask "What did you do in school today?" and your child answers "Nothing," ask more specific questions based on what you already know. Even if this further probing doesn't get you much information, you're still telling your child that you care about school (Claire Safran, *Reader's Digest,* September, 1985).

Discussing the Role of Education in Career Choices

Ask your child what careers sound interesting, and use this opportunity to discuss the wide range of career choices available. Use his answer as a basis to explore and discuss the education required for a particular career. Have these discussions periodically, since your child's career choices are likely to change as he matures. By focusing on the role of education in career choices, you can emphasize the critical role education plays in your child's adult life.

Discussing Successful People

Discuss with your child successful people from all walks of life. Include not only celebrities and other people in the public eye, but also successful neighbors, friends, or relatives, such as an older child who is going off to college and whom your child admires. Use such examples to show the importance of hard work and education in achieving goals and being successful.

Through discussions about people he respects, your child can see the importance of a good education to success in whatever he chooses to do.

Pointing Out the Advantages of a Good Education

When suitable topics come up in conversation, use the opportunity to mention the advantages an education can provide. For example, when people apply for an interesting and challenging job, the person with more formal education has a better chance of being hired. Likewise, when a person makes decisions in daily life, the more he knows, the better his chance of making the best decision. Help your child understand that, in general, the better a person's education, the better his chances for future success.

INSTILLING RESPECT FOR LEARNING

1. Always show a respect for education.

2. Make school an important topic of conversation in your home.

3. Discuss with your child the role of education in career choices.

4. Discuss with your child the importance of learning and education in the lives of successful people.

5. Point out the advantages an education can provide.

Fostering Independence and Self-Direction

As your child matures, he'll need to take increasing responsibility for his schoolwork. By helping him develop good study habits and skills, you can provide the foundation for self-directed learning. However, your child needs to develop self-initiative so that he can use the study skills and habits on his own. When he enters college, job training, or a career, you might not be available to assist him.

Involving Your Child

Throughout this book, we have encouraged you to help your child. However, to promote his independence and self-direction, you should always involve him in developing and deciding on study times, a place to study, study skills, motivation methods, or anything else related to schoolwork. He will then learn what study habits and skills are useful and how to motivate himself. Eventually, he will be able to make these decisions for himself, without your direction and help.

Gradually Reducing Your Help

Another way to help your child become a self-directed, independent learner is to have him gradually do more and more himself, with less and less help from you for such tasks as organizing his study location, collecting reference books, and developing study goals. That is, gradually reduce your involvement from year to year and reward your child every time he takes on more responsibility. Eventually, you'll just have to check to see that he is doing what he needs to and perhaps make a few suggestions. With your help, your child can gradually become independent in both organizing and carrying out school-related activities.

Encouraging Independence and Problem Solving

Always encourage your child to do things on his own whenever he can. For instance, if he doesn't know the meaning of a word, encourage and, if necessary, show him how to look it up in the dictionary. Or, if he doesn't know how to work a set of math problems, encourage him to either reread the directions in the book or see how another textbook explains how to do them.

Don't assume that you must always explain. Instead, direct your child to figure things out on his own. In this way, he'll reduce the need to come to you for help when he has problems and will be a more independent, self-directed learner.

Always be ready to help when necessary, but remember, you want to foster independence and self-direction even when you're helping.

A POINT TO PONDER

The difference between children who are self-motivated to succeed in school and those who are not is often their under-standing of what causes success or failure. Helping your child recognize that achievements are usually the result of hard work can help provide the inner motivation he needs. That is, children who believe that it is hard work, not luck or innate ability, that determines success or failure in school are more likely to be self-motivated.

Materials and Equipment that Foster Independence

You can help your child become a more independent learner by helping him learn to use study materials and equipment that provide guidance and feedback. For instance, programmed books on some subjects explain key concepts or show how to do something step-by-step, and provide immediate feedback on whatever your child comprehends about the subject.

Other materials and equipment can also foster independent learning. A dictionary or thesaurus can help your child with spelling, word meanings, and synonyms. A simple calculator can enable him to check math homework problems. A typewriter with a programmed spelling memory can tell him when he makes a spelling error. A home computer can help him in a variety of ways. He can also use a tape recorder for recording directions from class so that he can listen to them as well as read them, or for playing recordings of stories or pronunciations of foreign language words. Encyclopedias can provide your child with a wealth of information.

Such materials or equipment can enable your child to study independently, rather than having to rely on you for help. If you can't afford to buy some of the materials or equipment your child needs, try schools and libraries—many have such items that he can either use there or check out to take home.

FOSTERING INDEPENDENCE AND SELF-DIRECTION

1. Always involve your child in developing and deciding on his approach to schoolwork.

2. Gradually increase your child's level of responsibility for studying while decreasing your own involvement.

3. Encourage your child to either figure out or find answers to his questions rather than simply answering them yourself.

4. Help your child learn to use educational materials and equipment that can foster his independence.

To succeed in school and in life, all children need to learn independence and self-direction. Parents can foster these qualities in their child by involving him in making study plans, by gradually offering less help while rewarding his self-initiative and responsibility, and by helping him acquire study equipment and materials that give him guidance.

Conclusion

Motivation and self-direction are critical to your child's success throughout his educational career. You can foster these important qualities in him, thereby increasing his chances for ongoing school success.

Managing School-Related Stress

In the past few decades, stress has become one of the most serious problems children face. People of all ages have always had to cope with some degree of stress, but in today's increasingly complex world, the number and severity of stress factors facing children have risen dramatically.

Much of children's stress relates to their education. To help your child succeed in school, you need to recognize stress and help your child learn to deal with it productively.

What Is Stress?

Stress is caused by the strain and pressures of daily life. Personal or emotional stress is often caused by expectations, responsibilities, or social pressures. Most school-related stress is of this type. Environmental or physical stress, on the other hand, is often triggered by noise, pollution, or poor nutrition.

Stress in school is not necessarily bad. Problems arise when a child feels more stress than she can cope with, in which case she might show symptoms such as irrational fears, bed-wetting, rashes, overeating, nail biting, or forms of escape, such as drug or alcohol use, or even tendencies toward suicide.

Just as too much stress can be harmful, so can too little. If you constantly protect your child from all stress, she will never reap the benefits of healthy levels of stress or learn how to safely deal with too much stress.

A reasonable amount of stress will actually help your child succeed in school. It will motivate her to achieve and make her more creative and productive.

To succeed in school, your child must learn to harness the positive energy that stress creates. At the same time, she must learn to reduce unhealthy levels of stress that could detract from both her school achievement and her general feelings of well-being.

A key to healthy child development is controlling the amount of stress that your child experiences. If the childhood stresses increase gradually, your child can probably learn to control and cope with them. Problems arise when a child is faced with a dramatic increase in stress and has not yet developed the ability to deal with it.

What Are the Signs of Excessive Stress?

Some of the most common signs of too much stress in children are listed below. Remember, however, that nearly all children—whether they are experiencing too much stress or not—show at least some of these signs at various points. So don't be alarmed if your child shows a few of these signs temporarily. It's only when she displays a number of them over a period of time that you need to look for stresses that might be threatening her well-being.

- nail biting
- difficulty concentrating
- teeth grinding
- compulsive ear, hair, or clothes pulling
- poor eating or sleeping
- stuttering
- excessive eating or sleeping

- excessive crying
- headaches
- unusual mood changes
- neck or back pains
- sharp decline in school achievement
- bed-wetting
- stomach upset or vomiting
- ulcers

- listlessness
- impatience and sense of urgency
- irrational fears or anxiety
- frequent boasting of superiority
- thumb sucking
- nervous laughter
- demanding constant perfection
- loss of interest in school, family, or appearance
- excessive worrying or nervousness
- withdrawal from daily activities
- dislike of school
- downgrading self or feelings of unworthiness
- becoming accident-prone
- difficulty getting along with friends
- excessive attention-seeking activity, tension, or alertness
- nightmares
- easily startled
- frequent urination or diarrhea
- use of alcohol or drugs
- frequent daydreaming or retreating from reality
- rashes

In general, children react to excessive stress in one of two ways. They either worry a lot and withdraw or become very tense, nervous, and alert. A child who is tense, has nervous energy, and is constantly "on the run" can be suffering just as much as one who is worried, tired, and withdrawn.

If your child persistently displays some of the physical signs listed above (for example, headaches, neck or back pain, fatigue, or stomach upset), take her to your family physician for a complete physical examination. You don't want to mistakenly attribute her problem to stress if it has a physical cause. However, excessive stress is a more common problem among children than was once believed, and it is essential to recognize it and deal with it when it does occur.

Finally, if you see any indication that your child might have a serious problem, take her to a qualified counselor. You can usually start with her school counselor.

What Are the Sources of Excessive Stress?

The potential sources of stress are numerous. Since children's personalities differ, no two children react to stress factors in the same way. Some children, for example, can handle a hectic schedule with little or no stress, while others feel stressed by a seemingly moderate schedule of activities. However, the child with the hectic schedule might get overly stressed by some other factor, such as the need to be accepted by a large number of people. The causes of stress are often complex and difficult to detect, and excessive stress is usually caused by a combination of factors.

Pressure to Perform

Children have always felt pressure to do well in school from parents, teachers, and society in general. However, children now face greater pressure to achieve because of the current focus on excellence in education and the decline in jobs for people without a good education.

Stress-related problems do *not* stem from requiring students to work harder. Most children can work hard and feel very little pressure by giving up just a few minor outside activities. Problems occur when children are asked to perform *beyond* their capabilities. When a child works hard but simply can't perform at the level her parents and teachers expect, she can feel unhealthy, debilitating stress.

Some children just don't have the ability they need to meet basic academic standards. The vast majority of children, however, have the ability but haven't learned the study skills they need to achieve high standards.

Pressure to Compete

Children compete against each other from the time they enter school until the time they finish. They must compete for grades, friends, and their teachers' attention. The pressure of competition can cause excessive stress for some children, particularly if their parents constantly pressure them to "win" or be on top.

Pressure to Be Accepted

Most children feel a real need to be accepted. They want to be liked by their teachers and by other children. When this need becomes exaggerated, they can experience excessive stress.

Pressure to Adapt

Every year most children change classes, get new teachers, or meet new classmates. Thus, every year they must adapt to new pressures to compete, succeed, be accepted, and make friends. A young child who has just started school or an older student who has changed schools faces even more pressure to adapt. Adapting to new people and new situations can be stressful to almost anyone, including children.

Pressure to Do Too Much

Some children place undue pressure on themselves by getting involved in too many things—extracurricular activities, volunteer work, part-time jobs, hobbies—on top of their study schedules. Their lives then become hectic, and they might feel confused and frustrated, leading to excessive stress.

How Can You Help Your Child Reduce or Prevent Stress?

You can take several steps to help your child reduce or prevent stress; some of them might also help her cope with unavoidable stress.

Establishing Predictable Routine

As we discussed earlier, help your child develop a homework schedule, rules for doing assignments, and a study area with the tools and equipment she needs. Also, help her develop a schedule for other daily activities that she believes are important. A good schedule can help your child feel secure about what is expected of her, which in turn will reduce both her planning time and her chances of making mistakes when she schedules other activities. A predictable routine reduces stress because it helps your child clearly understand daily activities and perceive them as nonthreatening.

Setting Personal Goals for School Achievement

Your child can reduce stress by learning to set personal goals for school achievement. She should base these goals on her own needs, abilities, and interests rather than on what other children are achieving.

Too often, parents and school put pressure on children to compete with their peers and strive to be the "best." This is both unhealthy and unrealistic, since all children differ in their skills, abilities, and interests.

Encouraging children to compete against one another not only ignores their individuality, but also dooms the vast majority to failure. Instead, help your child develop challenging yet realistic goals related to her own abilities, needs, and interests. You want her to strive for top performance, but in harmony with her own abilities.

As your child achieves her goals, she can feel satisfied about reaching them and can then go on to develop more challenging goals. You can help her reduce excessive stress by basing your expectations not on *other* children's abilities or personalities but on her own.

A POINT TO PONDER

Always view your child and her accomplishments as unique. Try not to compare her work with that of another child. Every child is different, and comparisons with others might make your child feel bad about her abilities and cause her to lose her motivation to learn and succeed.

Setting Up a Realistic Daily Schedule

You can help control your child's stress by working with her to develop a realistic daily schedule. A common source of excessive stress is overplanning, planning to do more in a given time than is realistic.

Make sure you allow time for preparation, travel, resting, and thinking. Also, leave some time for unexpected events or forgotten chores, so that a surprise phone call, cleaning up after a pet's mischief, or going to the library for a forgotten book won't leave the day's schedule in total disarray and create unnecessary stress over unaccomplished goals.

Building a Positive Self-Image

You can also help reduce unnecessary stress by helping your child develop her self-esteem and a positive self-image. Your child needs to recognize her worth as a person.

Too often, children spend a lot of energy and feel a lot of anxiety and stress because they compare themselves with others. You can help by being careful, as noted in the previous section, not to compare your child's achievements with those of others. Instead, praise her for her unique efforts and achievements. Helping your child focus on her worth and potential can improve her self-esteem, thereby reducing her stress. (See Chapter 6 for other ways to improve your child's self-esteem.)

When your child learns that she is a worthwhile person regardless of how she compares with others, she will focus more energy and positive thoughts on school and doing the best she can.

Helping Others

Some children feel stressed because they get too caught up in their own lives—their situations and achievements and worrying about acceptance by others.

Help your child counteract this type of unhealthy stress by encouraging her to help others. Perhaps she could get involved in programs for tutoring younger children or reading to people in hospitals or nursing homes. Even if your child is having difficulties herself, she can and should help others. Not only will she be able to practice school-related skills, but she'll also find her attention drawn away from herself and toward the needs of others. Helping others will give her more confidence, since it's one of the best ways to build people's self-esteem.

A POINT TO PONDER

Are you inadvertently putting undue stress on your child? Do you contribute to her stress by being hurried and anxious yourself? Barbara Barker, in a recent issue of *Learning,* suggests that parents practice stress management techniques themselves. Stress is contagious; parents communicate their own anxieties, pressures, and fears to their children. Therefore, it's important to learn to manage your stress, not only for your own sake, but for your child's (Barbara Barker, *Learning,* January, 1987). Try practicing the things discussed in this chapter.

Separating Unhealthy Peer Pressure

School, which is a social as well as a learning environment, can produce considerable stress through peer pressure. Pressures to conform to other children's behavior begin as early as preschool and intensify as your child moves into her teens.

Many forms of peer pressure seem frivolous and sometimes bothersome, including hairstyles, clothing, and slang. These demands are generally harmless and will cycle in and out of style.

However, some types of peer pressure are destructive and dangerous. These include such things as drugs, alcohol, vandalism, joyriding, or hitchhiking. These activities are dangerous for your child and others.

Whenever your child stands up to peer pressure, she will feel stress and conflict. You can help her by being tolerant of harmless peer pressures and by teaching her how to recognize pressures that are dangerous. Then she'll know that you don't expect her to go against peer standards or fads as a general rule, but only when they involve such critical issues as drugs, alcohol, and illegal activities.

Choosing a Healthy Diet

Diet can affect how children behave. A child's diet can contribute to overactivity or to fatigue, either of which can cause unnecessary stress. Poor diet can also exaggerate a child's reactions to even moderate levels of stress.

You can help by making more fruits, vegetables, and whole grains available at home. Avoid foods with a lot of caffeine (particularly soda), refined sugars, salt, and saturated fats. Also, help your child make a habit of taking a multivitamin and eating a healthy breakfast each day before going to school.

In addition, teach your child to recognize and eat healthy foods when she's away from home. Good choices include caffeine-free drinks, fresh and dried fruits, low-fat foods, and snacks with little or no sugar.

Your child's physical well-being can go a long way in preventing stress from interfering with her school performance.

Increasing Awareness of Stress

If your child feels anxious, uneasy, or depressed, she, like most children, won't know exactly what is causing these feelings. She can reduce or prevent feelings of stress if she learns to recognize and understand them.

Teach your child to understand and deal with school-related stress as early as possible. For instance, talk about what she might experience on her first day at school or at a new school. Potential sources of stress would include meeting new classmates and teachers, learning new rules and schedules, and finding out where things are in the building. By talking about such situations before they arise, you can prepare her for them and make her feel more comfortable and secure. She'll know what to expect, which will give her the self-confidence she needs to handle the situation.

Don't be afraid to discuss stress with your child. You can share your own thoughts about stress and how it can sometimes even be helpful. You might also talk about the causes of stress and the warning signs of too much stress. Finally, teach your child how to use this book's suggestions, so she can learn to deal with stress productively.

PREVENTING OR REDUCING STRESS

Help your child:

1. Develop a predictable routine for school-related tasks.

2. Set school-achievement goals that fit her unique interests, needs, and capabilities.

3. Organize a realistic schedule of daily activities.

4. Recognize her worth as a person and help her develop self-esteem.

5. Focus attention on the needs and interests of others.

6. Recognize and avoid destructive or dangerous peer pressure.

7. Maintain a healthy diet.

8. Understand stress and its causes and learn to deal with it effectively.

How Can You Help Your Child Cope with Stress?

The best approach is to help your child prevent or reduce stress. Sometimes, however, high levels of stress are inevitable—for example, at examination time, when she first enters a new school, or when she must speak in public. In such cases, your child must learn to cope with the stress.

You can teach your child a number of strategies for dealing with school-related stress.

Nutrition

When your child faces a high degree of stress, encourage her to increase her intake of foods with vitamin C. Your body doesn't store vitamin C, and since it's a water soluble vitamin (that is, it's washed out of the body regularly), periods of stress can cause a vitamin C deficiency. Encourage your child to eat lots of citrus fruits, tomatoes, potatoes, and green leafy vegetables during stressful periods.

Exercise

All children need physical exercise, but it's especially important for children under stress. If your child seems stressed, but tends to spend her spare time in sedentary activities (watching television, talking on the phone, reading, or playing board games), make sure she includes physical exercise in her daily schedule. (This approach isn't necessary if your child gets plenty of exercise during her free time, in physical education class, or on the school playground.)

Even if exercise is scheduled, it should be fun and relaxing. It shouldn't become just another chore, or it will lose some of its value for reducing stress.

If your child doesn't enjoy physical exercise, suggest a host of different activities and then support whatever choices she makes. She might, for example, choose ice or roller skating, sledding, skiing, bowling, basketball, football, baseball, bicycling, dancing, or walking. Whatever she chooses, give her lots of encouragement and support.

If your child must stay inside during bad weather, take her to an indoor exercise area, such as a basketball court or swimming pool, or set aside space in your basement or garage for roller skating, hopscotch, gym equipment, or a trampoline.

Vigorous daily exercise is an important habit for your child to develop. It will benefit both her physical health and her ability to cope with stress.

Pleasant Breaks

If your child's schedule is increasingly hectic, help her learn to cope with her daily stress by suggesting and encouraging pleasant breaks. We all need breaks from our daily routines, and children under stress need them even more.

Nonstressful activities might be as simple as a short popcorn break, playing with a pet, or spending time on a hobby. When she has more time, a picnic, fishing trip, or short vacation can help reduce tension even more.

Occasional breaks can be very healthy, but too many breaks can increase stress rather than decrease it. They can interfere with study schedules and completing important assignments. Unfinished assignments and failure, in turn, heighten stress.

Friendships

A school friend is someone with whom your child can share ideas, feelings, and experiences. Friends can help your child understand and solve problems, be study partners, and help clarify school assignments. Likewise, they can help her feel secure in school-related situations. In short, friends are a critical part of your child's support system and can help her considerably in coping with daily stress.

Because school friendships are so critical to your child's well-being, and to the reduction of stress, encourage them by welcoming your child's friends into your home. Perhaps your child could invite a friend to go on a family outing or stay overnight, or could stay overnight with a friend's family. Do whatever you can to help your child develop close school friendships; their importance for coping with stress can't be overestimated. (See Chapter 6 for other ideas for helping your child form friendships.)

Parental Support

Not only is support from friends important to your child, so is your unconditional acceptance and support. Support from a warm, understanding parent is critical to your child's ability to deal with stress.

Parental support doesn't simply mean just providing money and physical necessities. To cope with stress, your child needs support that goes beyond providing adequate food, clothing, shelter, balanced meals, supervision, and transportation. Most important is the emotional support of a parent who cares, listens to concerns, tries to understand problems, and provides help, acceptance, and love regardless of school performance. Sometimes just a hug can tell your child that she's important to you and can provide the support she needs to cope with a difficult situation.

Being a good listener is one of the best ways to show your support. In fact, taking the time to listen is critical. Any child, especially one under stress, needs to know that you're sincerely interested in her feelings. Make time for your child to talk with you privately and uninterrupted. Parents who take the time to listen provide the support their children need to solve problems, find alternatives, or simply relieve stress by sharing their concerns.

Because many children can't articulate their needs and wants, you need to create a receptive atmosphere, ask questions, and to always keep the lines of communication open. By setting aside time to talk with your child, you can convince her that you are willing to listen and help her learn to solve problems. Be sure to talk about *your child's,* and *not your,* concerns about her behavior or school performance.

Despite any failure or difficulties in her daily school activities, your child needs to maintain her self-esteem and feelings of self-worth and acceptance. You can help by creating a caring and supportive family atmosphere. Only a loving, caring parent can provide the type of support that's needed.

WHAT IS THE WORST THING THAT COULD HAPPEN?

When something is really worrying your child, ask her "What is the worst thing that could happen?" In an article in *Reader's Digest* (July 1986), Antoinette Saunders and Bonnie Remsberg explained how to ask this question and what your child might gain.

"Okay, let's talk about this. What's the worst thing that could happen?" Treat your child's fear with respect. After she has answered, ask, "All right, what could you do to handle it?" This shows your confidence in her ability to cope.

Once the worst thing that could happen is out in the open, it will lose its mystique. You'll see your child's panic drain away almost as if by magic. The problem won't be solved yet; indeed, it might be a problem over which your child has no control. Just having your child say the unsayable, however, often takes away the problem's menace, especially when you listen with a loving and receptive ear.

Time Alone

Sharing time with others is beneficial, but everyone needs some time alone each day. Spending quiet time alone can strengthen your child's ability to cope with daily stress.

Time alone can provide your child with a period that's as stress-free as possible, when she isn't expected to accomplish anything and isn't exposed to social pressure from anyone—family, peers, or authority figures. She can sit and think, read for fun, daydream, or relax in a warm bath.

Some children spend quiet time alone regularly. If your child does not, however, you might find it difficult at first to get her to try it—especially if she gets caught up in a hectic schedule of school activities, sports, friends, and family life.

If your child is used to constant stimulation from others, she might at first feel anxious and bored. However, as she learns to adapt to a quiet, relaxed, private setting, she'll find that these quiet times reduce her feelings of stress and, in turn, increase her tolerance for stress at other times.

"You Are Not Alone"

When children are faced with a great deal of stress, they often forget that they are not alone. They aren't aware that many other people experience just as much or more stress in their daily lives. This sense of isolation can lead to self-pity and a feeling that life is cruel and unfair.

Such reactions to stress are damaging. Your child might feel that everything that happens is out of her control and that it's no use trying to make things better—feelings that only heighten stress.

You can help your child avoid such an attitude by reminding her that all children and adults experience stress and that she can learn ways to either avoid or deal with it. You might also want to make her aware that there are children who, for various reasons, face even more pressures in everyday life than she does. Realizing that she is not alone in experiencing stress can be a big help.

Positive Thinking

Every situation has both good and bad aspects, so encourage your child to think positively and look for the good rather than the bad. Explain that a positive thinker sees a glass as half full, not half empty. Positive thinking can help your child feel better about her daily experiences.

One parent-and-child sharing activity that encourages positive thinking is the "Good Night Formula." Each night before your child goes to bed, make sure you and she tell each other three things: 1) one good thing you like about yourself, 2) one thing you felt good about that happened during the day, and 3) something you are looking forward to tomorrow. This exercise provides practice in focusing on the good things in daily life.

Consistency

Consistency in the expectations, rules, and standards you set for your child will also help her cope with stress. Consistency in home discipline is important to building an atmosphere of security and trust. Children look for limits, and once they find them, they can relax and feel secure knowing what you expect of them.

Relaxation Techniques

One of the most common strategies for coping with stress is the use of relaxation techniques. Children can learn many of these techniques. Two of the easiest are visual imagery and muscle relaxation.

A. Visual Imagery

Ask your child to:

(1) Get into a comfortable position.

(2) Pretend that her eyelids are getting very heavy and let them gradually close.

(3) Take a deep breath through her nose, hold it for a few seconds, and then release it.

(4) Imagine a pretty, quiet, peaceful place, such as a beach, meadow, or garden, and then picture herself in it. (Make sure it's a place your child is familiar with.)

(5) Smell the fresh, sweet smells of the place, and feel a light breeze blowing and the sunshine falling on her face and arms.

(6) Notice how good she feels and how happy she is to be there and to walk around, sit, or lie down there for a few moments.

(7) Begin coming back from that place while counting from one to five.

(8) Open her eyes, stand up, and stretch, trying to touch the sky or ceiling. (Or she can use another stretching exercise.)

After this short "vacation," your child should be more relaxed and ready to go on with her daily activities.

B. Muscle Relaxation

Ask your child to:

(1) Lie down on her back or in another comfortable position.

(2) Pretend her eyelids are getting heavy and close her eyes.

(3) Take a deep breath through her nose, hold it for a moment, and then exhale, letting all the tenseness in her muscles blow out of her body with the old air.

(4) Raise her right leg and tense the muscles in it. Feel all the muscles tighten until the leg gets tired. Put the leg down and relax the muscles, feeling them loosening up.

(5) Repeat the directions in number 4 with the following parts of her body: left leg, right arm, left arm, stomach, chest, shoulders and neck, and head.

(6) After tensing and relaxing all her muscles, picture a circle in her mind and follow the line of the circle with her eyes, going around it three times in one direction and three times in the other.

(7) Be still and breathe normally for a few minutes, then get up, and continue with her day.

Once your child has practiced this exercise with you, she will soon be able to relax in a sitting position and will no longer need to lift each body part. Many children also learn to relax their muscles without first tightening them.

COPING WITH STRESS

Help your child:

1. Increase her intake of food with vitamin C during periods of high stress.

2. Schedule and enjoy vigorous physical exercise every day.

3. Plan periodic, pleasant, nonstressful breaks from her daily routine.

4. Develop a close friendship with a schoolmate.

5. Increase her self-esteem, with your acceptance and support.

6. Spend some quiet time alone each day.

7. Be a positive thinker, looking at the good aspects of any situation.

8. Learn and practice relaxation techniques.

Conclusion

Stress can serve as either an enemy or a friend in your child's quest to succeed in school. Too often, the detrimental effects of too much daily stress can overpower your child, causing her to feel anxious and unhappy and interfering with her school success.

With your help, your child can control these detrimental effects by learning how to reduce and cope with stress.

Overcoming Learning and Behavior Problems

Learning and behavior problems, such as a poor self-concept, hyperactivity, and uncooperative behavior, interfere with school success. Your child can overcome most common learning and behavior problems by developing good study attitudes, habits, and skills. If your child has any such problems, therefore, it's essential to help him learn the skills discussed throughout this book. Many parents (and educators) make the mistake of overlooking the basic skills for doing well in school while searching for a magical cure for specific problems. Unfortunately, they rarely, if ever, find one.

Hyperactivity

The Problem

Some children are always "on the go." They seem to be in motion constantly. This extremely high activity level can interfere with their ability to stick to a task long enough to finish it. If your child has this problem, you can take certain steps at home to help.

Recommendations

The main schoolwork-related goal to strive for with a hyperactive child is to help him organize tasks so that he can complete them. The satisfaction and rewards he achieves by completing school tasks will gradually help motivate him to finish tasks rather than jumping from one to another.

(1) Help your child break homework assignments into several smaller tasks. For example, he can divide a fifteen-problem math assignment into three five-problem tasks, with a two- or three-minute "active" break scheduled after each set. This approach also gives him the satisfaction of completing three tasks instead of only one.

(2) Divide his study time across different subjects so he won't have to work on the same subject for a long time. That is, have him complete a small task in math, then go on to reading, then go back to math, then to science, and so on.

(3) As your child gets better at completing small tasks, slowly increase the size of the tasks until he is able to finish entire assignments. Be sure, however, that he is successfully *completing* the tasks. Don't increase the size of the tasks more quickly than he can tolerate.

(4) Help your child develop a consistent routine for finishing homework assignments and other school-related tasks. This means approaching his schoolwork in a highly organized manner and doing it the same way each study session. Such a routine is critical for a hyperactive child. It means that he'll be less likely to get sidetracked and will develop an automatic series of steps to help him complete his work. In addition, the routine will make him feel secure about what he needs to do next, so he doesn't get anxious or overstimulated trying to figure it out.

(5) A simple strategy that helps some hyperactive children is a change in diet. Help your child recognize and eliminate those foods that contain stimulants, such as caffeine, sugar, and chocolate. Check with his physician for specific recommendations. Dietary changes alone won't help your child succeed in school—he still must develop good study skills—but they can help reduce the physical overstimulation and anxiety that lead to school problems.

(6) Some hyperactive children benefit from drug treatment or allergy desensitization under the direction of a physician. Drugs

such as stimulants, tranquilizers, megavitamins, corticosteroids, antihistamines, and anticonvulsants sometimes help; however, side effects and overuse of these drugs have caused many parents, educators, and physicians to view them with disfavor. Hyperactivity is sometimes caused by allergies (for example, intolerance to common foods, food coloring, additives, dusts, chemical fumes, or pollen), so allergy treatment has also become increasingly useful. Both drug treatment and allergy desensitization, however, must be supervised by knowledgeable medical personnel. They must also be supplemented by developing good study schedules and motivation if your child's school performance is to improve.

For other suggestions on helping a hyperactive child, see the section on "Inattention and Daydreaming" later in this chapter.

Memory Problems or Forgetfulness

The Problem

Some children seem unable to remember what schoolwork they are supposed to do each day. They often also have difficulty remembering what they study.

Recommendations

(1) Explain to your child why he needs to remember something. People remember things better when they have a good reason.

(2) Be sure your child understands anything he needs to remember. As we noted in Chapter 3, it's much easier to remember things you understand.

(3) Help your child form a mental image of anything he needs to remember. It's easier, for example, to remember a mental image of a milk carton than to remember the word "milk." Similarly, it's easier to remember a mental image of Paul Revere in eighteenth-century clothes riding to warn of the British advance than to remember a paragraph describing the event. Thus, encourage your child to form mental images of whatever he studies.

(4) Teach your child how to use association to improve his memory skills. Association enables you to recall one item when another reminds you of it. Encourage your child to associate a word, idea, formula, date, or anything he has trouble remembering

with something he remembers easily. One of the authors, for example, remembers Thomas Jefferson's birthday (April 13, 1743) because his birthday is April 13, 1943, two hundred years later.

(5) Encourage your child to recite to himself important material that he needs to remember. Nothing improves memory better than simple repetition. Have him also try reciting something thirty minutes to an hour after he learns it, to see whether he still remembers it. If he doesn't, he'll need to refresh his memory.

(6) Discourage your child from studying two similar subjects together. Instead, have him study a dissimilar subject in between. For example, he shouldn't study chemistry right after algebra—he might have trouble remembering material from one subject without confusing it with material from the other.

(7) Help your child form the habit of making notes or lists of things to remember. Making lists will be easier and more pleasant if you buy or make him personalized notepads. If the list includes things your child needs to do, encourage him to check off each task when he completes it and then read the list to see what his next task is.

If the list includes study items to remember, such as spelling words, history dates, or foreign language words, encourage your child to review the list several times a day. Also, you might want to ask to see the list periodically and check off all the items he can remember. Reviewing the list consistently and repeatedly can help your child remember what is on it. His memory for other things will also improve, since the best way to improve one's memory is to try to remember things.

(8) Furnish him with special signs or notebooks to help him remember things. For instance, you might put a sign in his study area to remind him to collect the books and tools he needs before he starts studying. Similarly, he might keep a notebook for homework assignments divided into columns that list each assignment by date, subject, task, book, page, and when due. This will not only help him remember homework assignments, it will also help him learn how to organize and remember important tasks—a lesson that could benefit him throughout his life.

(9) Use various cues such as rhymes, riddles, songs, and phrases to help your child remember things. Examples include the *A-B-C* song for remembering the alphabet, and the phrase "When two vowels go walking, the first one does the talking" for remembering that when two vowels come together the second one is silent. Children who have problems writing the letters *b* and *d* can remember how to form them by learning to spell the word "bed." They can visually make the word into a bed. Then, if they reverse either the *b* or the *d*, they'll know because the word won't look like a bed anymore.

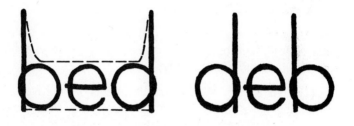

Your child can tell direction more easily by holding up both hands with the fingers extended and the palms facing away. The thumb and index fingers of his left hand will make the letter *L*.

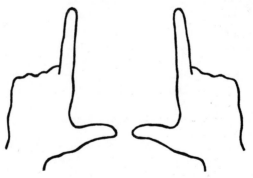

You can find these memory cues, or mnemonic devices, in books, but encourage your child to make up his own. Cues that he makes up himself will be easier to remember.

(10) Keep encouraging your child to remember. The more your child tries, the more his memory will improve with time. That is, your

child must use his memory, much like a muscle, in order for it to function at its best or improve.

Reading Difficulties

The Problem

Reading is the most important skill your child needs for studying and learning. From their early school years through high school and college, many children find reading to be a difficult problem. The difficulty is usually in reading fluently and for comprehension.

Recommendations

Serious reading problems usually require help from a reading specialist or teacher, but you can take a number of steps at home to help your child read more proficiently.

(1) Look for any small accomplishments or improvements in reading—this recognition might help your child learn to enjoy reading. Don't trigger negative feelings toward reading by putting too much pressure on your child to improve. Also, don't focus on mistakes or problems. You don't want your child to dislike reading.

(2) Try "paired reading." This exercise involves spending fifteen or thirty minutes each day reading with your child. To break your child's cycle of failure, emphasize success and praise, and make sure you help in a nonthreatening way. Make paired reading fun, rather than a form of work. Try the following:

- Sit down side by side on a sofa or any other comfortable place. Choose a quiet place, but not your child's regular study area. You want your child to view paired reading as enjoyable and recreational rather than as homework.

- At first, choose reading materials that are interesting to your child but below his school reading level. Simpler materials will help ensure that he'll find the reading easy, feel successful, and improve his reading fluency. As you read more and more with him, he'll want to try more challenging reading material, so gradually increase its difficulty.

- Take a relaxed, positive approach. Use library books instead of school readers, and allow your child to choose the books, as well as the time and duration of your paired reading period. (Give your child these choices, but don't give him a choice about whether or not to do paired reading.)

• If your child finds reading extremely difficult, try the following steps. First, read a passage or story to him and talk about the pictures, people, and events. Then, reread it, pointing out each word by running your finger under the line of print. Have your child follow along, looking at the words as you read. Third, reread the story together, stopping occasionally to let him read a word or finish a sentence on his own. As your child's proficiency and confidence increase, encourage him to do more of the reading and do less of it yourself.

• When your child reads to you, remember to praise him for such things as reading a sentence correctly, correcting himself after a mistake, and pronouncing a word correctly after you helped him. Don't make negative comments or focus on mistakes. If he reads a word incorrectly, prompt him with clues such as the meaning of the word. If he still doesn't get the word right, say the word yourself and then let him continue reading.

(3) Encourage your child to practice reading. Whether he uses paired reading or some other approach, he simply *must* practice to become a good reader. To encourage him, you need to emphasize reading in your home. Here are some things you can do:

• Be sure that you read magazines and books regularly. Parents who read set a model that influences their children's reading habits.

• Make regular trips to the library and take your child along. Library visits can become a shared activity that you both enjoy.

• Make reading part of your family's daily routine. If the circus is coming to your area, for example, or if your family is planning a trip, bring home books on these topics. Your child's enthusiasm for these events will spill over into reading about them, both before and afterwards.

• Use television to encourage your child's interest in reading. When he sees something on television that interests him, encourage him to read about it. For example, if he enjoyed a program about whales, find him some written material about whales. (For older children, *National Geographic* is a particularly valuable resource on animals and other cultures.) If he watches a show about a famous athlete or president whom he admires, check that person's biography or autobiography out of the library.

- Use the newspaper to encourage your child to read. When you come across an article that might interest him (for example, an article about squirrels in the park, Little League baseball, or a favorite celebrity's local concert), show it to your child and encourage him to read it. If he can't read the newspaper, read the article to him, pointing out any pictures and captions. This could help interest him in learning to read well enough to read the newspaper. Most children enjoy the comics sections, and even that can help refine his skills.

- Books make wonderful gifts. For special occasions, take your child to the bookstore and let him select a book. Giving a book as a gift helps emphasize that books are something special. You might also bring home books, comics, or magazines as treats when you go to the store or on a trip, instead of bringing home candy or toys. Keep in mind that gift books or magazines are for your child's enjoyment, to help him with motivation, practice, and reading fluency. Thus, choose ones that reflect your child's interests and that he would want to read. Some parents we know report that the favorite and most frequently read magazine in their child's library is *MAD* magazine—much to their chagrin. Some people view *MAD* as having little redeeming social value, but in these cases, it serves as an incentive for practicing reading.

- Make reading time a priority in your home. Some children and their families get involved in so many activities (for example, Scouts, guitar lessons, dancing lessons, part-time jobs) that they have little time left for reading. In fact, lack of time is one of the most frequently cited reasons for why children and adults don't read. If you want your child to be a good reader, you and he simply must make reading a high priority. Set aside some time for reading during the day. You could use this time for "paired reading," as discussed earlier, or for each person to read alone. It doesn't need to be a lot of time; fifteen or thirty minutes might be enough. And don't worry too much about what your child reads, especially when he is first starting out. Encourage any or all forms of reading that appeal to him.

- Chapter 9 offers suggestions for setting up a home atmosphere and activities that encourage reading. For more ideas, write to the International Reading Association, P.O. Box 8139, 800 Barksdale Road, Newark, Delaware 19711.

(4) Ensure that your child's reading material is interesting to him and appropriate for his age. To get material with a simple enough vocabulary for easy reading, parents too often end up with something below their child's age and interest level. Talk with your child's teacher or a librarian about "high-interest, low-vocabulary" books for your child.

(5) Find out whether your child comprehends what he reads. To do this in a friendly, nonthreatening way, discuss his reading with him. After you ask a few questions, both you and he will probably know whether he understands and remembers what he read. If he doesn't, encourage him to reread it. Children often devise their own ways to understand and remember when they're motivated to talk about their reading. (You might, however, want to give your child some ideas for improving his comprehension, such as those discussed in "Studying for Understanding," Chapter 3.)

(6) Remember to coordinate any assistance you provide at home with the reading program at your child's school. Let his teacher know what you are doing at home and ask for other suggestions.

Spelling Difficulties

The Problem

Some children find spelling very difficult. They are often reluctant to take essay tests, write papers, or do other school activities that require good spelling.

Recommendations

(1) Encourage your child to keep a personal notebook of words that give him trouble. Have him make up a list of words that he has misspelled in the past. Look over the list of common or recurrent errors and help your child practice spelling the words.

(2) Be sure to have your child's hearing thoroughly evaluated by an audiologist. Precise hearing is essential for comprehension and spelling.

(3) Encourage your child to learn the meanings of difficult-to-spell words. Knowing the meaning of a word might help him remember how to spell it.

(4) Be sure your child owns and uses a good dictionary. Also, as Francis Roberts recommended recently in *Parents Magazine*, (February 1987), try to provide him with a reference book such as *New Century 50,000 Words Divided and Spelled* (New Century Publishers, 1978). This book has long lists of words in alphabetical order and, for many people, is more useful than a dictionary for finding correct spellings.

(5) Have your child follow an eight-step plan to study troublesome words:

Step 1: Look up the meaning of the word in a dictionary or other source.

Step 2: Use the word in a sentence or two.

Step 3: Look carefully at the word that causes trouble.

Step 4: Copy the word exactly, noting all its features (for example, any prefixes or suffixes).

Step 5: Sound out the word.

Step 6: Cover the word, visualize it, and rewrite it from memory.

Step 7: Uncover the word and check the spelling.

Step 8: Spell the word quietly several times in order to hear it being spelled.

Have your child repeat these steps several times until he remembers how to spell troublesome words.

(6) Every chance you get, let your child try to spell words in a safe, nonthreatening environment. For example, encourage him to spell words during daily activities such as making out a grocery list. Be ready to help with spellings whenever necessary. Ongoing, daily practice in a relaxed environment is a good way to learn how to spell.

Uncooperative Behavior

The Problem

Some children are unwilling to cooperate with their parents in planning either a study schedule or other activities to help them do better in school. Other children might cooperate in planning but refuse to carry out what they plan. Whether uncooperative behavior shows up as stubbornness, laziness, or direct refusal, you must know how to deal with it.

Recommendations

(1) Help your child overcome his uncooperative behavior by making school success worth his effort. Review the suggestions on motivation in Chapter 4, since a lack of cooperation is often tied to poor motivation. You might also have your child earn at least part of his allowance by completing study goals or homework assignments. Or, as an alternative, have him earn certain privileges such as watching favorite television programs, playing in Little League ball, or using the telephone. The uncooperative child is often difficult to deal with, and you might need strong measures such as these to get him to study. You can hope that as soon as he becomes more successful in school, the natural benefits of studying (increased knowledge, satisfaction from a job well done, good grades) will take over and you'll no longer need these strong measures.

(2) Consider making a contract with your child; it's often an effective way of dealing with uncooperative behavior. In such a contract, your child might agree to do his schoolwork, and you might agree to let him do or get something he wants. That is, he earns what he wants by doing what you want. Note that such a contract is an exchange of behaviors, privileges, or goods, it is *not* bribery.

When you and your child develop a contract, be sure to define its terms clearly, especially the following:

- Your child's responsibilities (for example, being on time for study period). List them on a chart posted in his study area to remind him of what he needs to do.

- Your responsibilities. Specify what resources you will furnish to help your child fulfill his part of the contract, and what rewards you will provide when he does.

- Negative consequences that will occur if your child doesn't fulfill his part of the agreement. If you state negative consequences (for example, loss of his allowance, grounding for a weekend) ahead of time and involve your child in the decision, he'll more likely feel that the consequences are fair.

- A bonus clause listing extra rewards for complying with the agreement consistently. This will show your child the benefits of working on a regular basis.

- How you will monitor and administer the contract. For example, who will check to see whether both sides are fulfilling the contract? How will records be kept? Accomplishments rewarded?

- Be sure that you develop any such contract in cooperation with your child and that both you and he agree on the terms. Keep the contract brief, no more than a page long, and make sure you both sign it.

SAMPLE SCHOOLWORK CONTRACT

The following contract is an agreement between Jerry Smith and his parents, John and Cora Smith (Mom & Dad).

1. Jerry will study for one hour and a half every weekday evening immediately after supper. (An hour and a half on a weekend day or evening can be substituted for Friday if arranged with Dad ahead of time.)

2. Mom and Dad will allow Jerry to use the family computer, watch television, and talk on the phone for up to one hour (before 10:00 pm) for each homework session he completes. Mom and Dad will also provide quiet time when Jerry is doing homework.

3. When Jerry does not complete a homework session, he will not be allowed to play outside with his friends before supper the next day. Also, he will not earn the privilege of computer, TV, or phone time for any evening he does not finish his study time.

4. When Jerry completes his study sessions every weekday evening (five sessions in a row), he will receive $5.00, and on the weekend, he'll be allowed to go to a movie, skating, bowling, or a similar activity of his choice with his friends.

5. To monitor fulfillment of this contract, Mom or Dad will check off each study session on a chart as Jerry completes it. The chart will be posted in the study area and will include five study sessions per week. When a space is checked off, it means that Jerry has earned his hour of TV, computer, or phone time. When all five spaces for the week are checked, Jerry has earned his weekend bonus.

6. We agree to this contract.

_____

_____

_____

September 9, 1988

(3) Help your child relate his schoolwork to his own interests and hobbies. Children do schoolwork more willingly when they can apply it to real life. For example, encourage your child to relate his math problems to measuring for a building project, planting a garden, figuring out supplies for a party, or counting money to buy things. Or have him relate writing practice to writing a letter to a friend, spelling to making a grocery list, or science to looking at the weather and how it can affect a trip to the beach or a ball game. You can often overcome uncooperative behavior by making schoolwork relevant to your child's daily life.

(4) Try to understand why your child is being uncooperative. You need to deal with uncooperative behavior in a straightforward manner, but make sure you also try to find out what's causing it. Any number of reasons might be involved. For example, some children are afraid they are going to fail no matter how hard they try, so they see no reason to keep trying. Others see no value in doing well in school; they believe they can do well in life without a good education. Still others believe their friends will reject them if they succeed in school.

Listening to your child and trying to understand his point of view will give you the best chance of pinpointing the real reason for his uncooperative behavior. Try to put yourself in his place and see how he feels. By doing that, you'll have a better idea of how to help him become more cooperative. Open and honest communication is critical to eliminating uncooperative behavior as well as many other learning and behavior problems.

A POINT TO PONDER

A few parents have asked us, "What if my child is gifted or has a visual, hearing, or severe reading disability? Shouldn't I be doing something about that instead of helping him set up a study schedule, learn good study skills, overcome problem behaviors, and so on?" If you suspect that your child has a disability or is gifted, you should get guidance from a qualified specialist. However, remember that disabled or gifted children also need a study schedule and good study skills and habits. *All* children need to learn the basic skills to do well in school. Thus, get the guidance from a qualified specialist, *but* also be sure to help your child learn the fundamentals for doing well in school.

Difficulty in Understanding

Problem

Some students seem to have extreme difficulty grasping and understanding what they study. That is, they seem unable to understand directions, explanations, or key concepts.

Recommendations

(1) When your child studies, have him separate out any material he doesn't understand and then have him reread it. Sometimes a second or third reading is all that he needs. (A common mistake many children make is to assume they only need to read assigned study material once. Actually, most serious schoolwork needs to be read several times.)

(2) Encourage your child to determine whether there is something else he needs to understand before he can figure out his current assignments. To solve some advanced math and science problems, for example, you must first understand more basic information or concepts. If you suspect that this is your child's problem, tell him to look at some introductory books on

the subject. Usually, a few pages or a small part of a chapter will provide the basic information he needs to know. For subjects that give your child trouble, try to keep on hand a few secondhand textbooks that are a year or two below his grade level.

(3) Have your child find some "simplified" books on the topic. As noted in Chapter 3, these books are available for subjects such as algebra, physics, chemistry, and foreign languages. You can find them in most well-stocked bookstores.

(4) When your child studies, encourage him to list any words or terms he doesn't clearly understand. Not understanding a term could hinder his overall comprehension. He can find definitions of these terms in the book's glossary or dictionary. Also, encourage him to list and look carefully at any formulas or principles that he must remember to understand and solve what he is studying.

(5) When possible, let your child work directly with what he is studying. For example, if he is learning about adding money, let him add real money. If you can't provide the real thing, do whatever you can to help make the subject real and concrete. If your child is studying French, for instance, give him pictures of people, maps, and other items related to France to make the country and its language seem more real.

(6) Encourage your child to divide anything he doesn't understand into parts. Sometimes children can get a better grasp on a difficult problem or passage if they break it down into small parts and study it part by part.

(7) If your child is having trouble with a math or science problem, have him carefully read the directions and explanations, and then formulate a hypothesis, or best guess, as to how to solve it. That is, have him write down or clearly picture how he *thinks* the problem *might* be solved. Then he can try to solve it. If he gets the wrong answer, have him modify his hypothesis and try again. By formulating a hypothesis about how to solve the problem, trying to solve it, modifying his hypothesis if it doesn't work, and trying again, your child approaches the problem in an orderly, systematic fashion. In solving problems, it's important to work toward the solutions systematically, not haphazardly.

(8) Have your child explain what he does and doesn't understand. Explaining something to another person sometimes helps children figure out what they don't understand.

(9) Encourage your child not only to read and talk about what he doesn't understand, but also to write it down or listen to himself talk about it on a tape recorder. The more ways he experiences the material, the more likely he is to grasp and understand it.

(10) Encourage your child to leave difficult material alone for a while and come back to it later. However, make sure he does this only after making a concerted effort to understand it.

See the first half of Chapter 3 for additional ways to help children understand what they study.

Dislike for School

The Problem

The two most common reasons for children not wanting to attend school are failure in school and lack of social acceptance or friendships. The focus of this book is on how helping your child succeed in school will help him overcome his dislike, if it is based on failure. However, you can help him in other specific ways if his problem is one of social acceptance.

School is a social environment, so children who have trouble with social acceptance find themselves at a disadvantage. Often such children don't develop a support system of school friends. This problem is particularly common among children who enter a new school, join a class in midyear, or tend to be quiet or withdrawn. School is much more enjoyable for children with a good social base.

Recommendations

(1) Encourage your child to invite a classmate on a fun family outing or trip. This will give the two of them time to get to know each other and have fun together.

(2) Encourage your child to join social and recreational groups such as Scouts, ball teams, summer camp, or dance classes, and provide whatever support he needs to participate. Seek out activities in which other children from his class are involved. These activities will enable your child to get to know his classmates outside of school and to form friendships that will carry over into school.

(3) Encourage your child to use your home as a gathering place for children from his school. Make a social area available in your home, get to know the children and invite them in, and give them refreshments and privacy. Let your neighbors know that their children are welcome and will be properly supervised while they have fun with their peers. If possible, have available recreational equipment such as a stereo, a pool table, darts, or other games.

(4) Consider meeting with your child's teacher or school counselor to ask about any special courses or tutoring programs in the school or community to help children with socialization problems—particularly if your child's problem is severe. Courses or tutoring can teach your child assertiveness and how to get along with others.

(5) Help your child improve his chances for developing friendships by working with him on skills that promote friendships. These skills include finding areas of compatibility with others, sharing, being a good listener, recognizing other people's accomplishments, helping and supporting others, seeing other people's points of view, smiling, being loyal and trustworthy, and handling problems fairly. Try discussing these skills with him, showing him how they work, and encouraging him to practice them.

By encouraging your child to use these skills around potential friends, you can help him develop and maintain friendships.

(6) When you encourage your child to form friendships, remember that more friends are not necessarily better than a few. One or a few classmates with whom your child can feel comfortable, confide, and share ideas and feelings can provide the support he needs for enjoyment, security, and success in school.

A POINT TO PONDER

When parents consistently set rules for their children that are very different from the rules other parents impose, their children may be viewed as different. As a result, other children might exclude them from some social activities. Bobby, for example, lives near the school and goes home for lunch every day, while all his classmates eat in the cafeteria; Jessica isn't allowed to play kickball or other running games at recess; Paul doesn't have much to say about the latest TV episode of *Family Ties* because his parents do not let him watch it.

This does *not* mean that the rules you have for your child can't be different from those of other parents. In fact, the difference might be necessary and desirable. Just make sure you consider what effects they might have on your child's social relationships and friendships (David Bjorklund and Barbara Bjorklund, *Parents Magazine*, May, 1987).

Poor Self-Concept

The Problem

Many children refuse to try new ideas or tackle difficult tasks because they believe they will fail. That is, they lack confidence in their own ability.

This problem is a major roadblock to achieving school success, since in school, children are constantly required to try more difficult material and tasks. Facing challenges is an integral part of learning.

Recommendations

If your child has a poor self-concept, the key to overcoming the problem is to have him repeatedly experience success in schoolwork and other learning tasks. Success breeds confidence and a good self-concept, while failure leads to a poor self-concept. You can help your child increase his success rate or at least minimize his failures.

(1) Recognize and praise even partial achievements. Your child doesn't need to complete an entire assignment or do everything correctly to experience success. For example, if he completes two of ten math problems correctly, be sure you praise him for the two correct problems before you help him figure out how to solve the other eight. When he gets a report card, praise his good or acceptable grades before you discuss his poor grades. After you recognize his achievements, then you can discuss the problems. However, make sure that any discussion of problems *always* includes things he can change. And be sure to close any discussion of problems by again praising his accomplishments.

(2) Arrange for your child to tutor another child. Most children who lack self-confidence are knowledgeable in at least one subject, and nothing can improve a child's self-esteem more than using his expertise to help someone else. Being in a teaching or helping role will make him feel successful. Even if he is not

strong in any particular subject, he can still tutor a younger child who knows less than he does. An extra benefit is that your child will probably increase his own knowledge of the subject, since the best way to learn about a subject is to teach it to someone else.

(3) To enhance or at least protect your child's self-concept, make sure you don't compare his achievements with those of other children. Instead, compare them with his own past achievements, challenging him to do better. Each child has different talents and abilities, so comparisons between children are unfair. If you compare your child with a peer who has more natural talent in a particular area, he might lose both his confidence in his own abilities and his motivation to succeed in school.

(4) Work with your child's teachers to make sure he has schoolwork that is challenging, but not beyond his abilities. His self-concept will suffer if he is constantly required to do schoolwork beyond his capabilities. You can also make sure that he has learning tasks to do at home that he can successfully complete and that you reward him when he does.

(5) Emphasize your child's strengths every chance you get. Give him ample opportunity to use his strengths so he can feel successful. For example, if he has trouble with most schoolwork but does well in math, let him use his math skills whenever possible in your family's daily life.

(6) If you help your child stick to a study schedule and learn good study skills, he will probably become successful in school. By paying attention to these fundamental principles, you'll help him develop a positive self-concept in his schoolwork.

A POINT TO PONDER

Every child's school successes should far outweigh his failures; however, failures are an inevitable, natural part of life. Therefore, your child needs to develop a productive attitude toward failure.

As one of our own wise parents has told us repeatedly, "If you never fail, you're probably not trying anything very challenging." That is, when you try new challenges, you can expect to fail occasionally and learn from your failures.

You can help your child's self-concept by explaining that everyone experiences failure. Teach him that successful people use failure as an opportunity to learn rather than as a sign of defeat. You don't want your child to experience failure too often, but he needs to know that it's sometimes inevitable when people are trying to do their best.

Inattention and Daydreaming

The Problem

Some children find it extremely difficult to concentrate on their schoolwork. They often get distracted or daydream. One father told us that his son always seemed to be staring off into space when he was supposed to be studying.

Recommendations

(1) Help your child eliminate any concerns or interests that might distract him during his study time. Before he studies, try to talk with him about the day's events and anything that is bothering him so he won't have them on his mind during study time. That will reduce the chance of his being distracted from his studying by worries, uncertainties, or excitement.

(2) Have your child work on one fairly short task at a time, and have him remove everything he doesn't need for that task from the top of his desk.

(3) Help your child remove any items from the study area that might catch his attention or encourage him to think about something other than schoolwork (for example, a phone, games, or hobby materials). See Chapter 2 for ideas on organizing a nondistracting study area.

(4) Encourage your child to use innovative study methods. For example, children who can't focus on particular words or sentences on a page because they get distracted by the other

words or sentences often find it helpful to draw a bold, heavy square around what they need to study. Some also use a plain sheet of paper as a cover sheet. Your child can use a cover sheet when reading a story or a word list or doing a page of math problems to cover the material he either just finished or hasn't read yet. A large index card with a space cut out can also help your child focus on a word, sentence, or math problem.

(5) Besides eliminating distractions, help your child increase his interest in and enjoyment of schoolwork. Children tend to pay more attention to things that interest them. Encourage your child to approach school assignments as challenging games. For example, have him try to beat his own record for time or accuracy in doing math problems or in making up funny sentences for spelling words. Also, help him relate what he learns in school to familiar things to make his study time more interesting and exciting. For example, if a neighbor recently visited Mexico and your child is studying Mexico, talk about what your neighbor saw, ate, experienced, and bought on the trip and how it compares with what the textbook says about the country.

(6) Talk to your child about the importance of topics he is studying. All children (and adults) concentrate better on topics they think are important. You might want to talk with teachers or various people in your community about the importance of the subjects your child is learning in school. Then you will be better able to discuss their relevance with your child.

(7) Use a timer to help your child practice concentrating. Set the timer for five or ten minutes and have your child begin his schoolwork. He must sit and concentrate on whatever he is studying until the bell rings. Gradually increase the time limit as his attention span improves.

(8) Try showing your child how athletes concentrate on a baseball game or tennis match. They often say to themselves, "Concentrate! Concentrate!" "I've got to keep my eye on the ball." When your child is doing his homework, he can practice saying such positive things to himself ("I can pay attention." "I can keep my mind on my work." "I can do it.").

(9) Try to be available during study time. If you are nearby, you can draw your child's attention back to his work if his interest wanes. Just a simple reminder can help him refocus his attention. Note that it's especially important to be available

during the first five or ten minutes. Many children waste a great deal of time settling down to a task, but once they get started, they can maintain their concentration. You can help your child get started simply by asking him what he needs to do first and having him show you his assignments.

(10) If your child has serious trouble attending to any task for very long, as in the case of hyperactivity, try breaking his study material into smaller units or his study time into shorter periods. Gradually increase the length of his tasks or study periods as his attention span improves.

Lack of Basic Ability

The Problem

Some children have trouble in school because they lack the basic ability to learn and understand material. This lack of ability might show up in only one subject area, or in all of them.

A WORD OF OPTIMISM

Children who seem to lack the basic ability to learn and succeed in school sometimes surprise their parents as well as teachers, school psychologists, counselors, and other experts. As the children mature, their apparent lack of ability might simply disappear. These children just seem to be late bloomers, that is, they start learning at a later age.

In fact, we know several people who at some point failed in school and were considered "slow." Later, they became successful in academic careers. One of the authors of this book failed the third and fourth grades and got poor grades throughout elementary school and most of high school. Later, however, he earned a doctorate and has authored many scientific papers and books.

We strongly recommend that you never give up on your child's education. Even if you feel your child truly lacks basic ability, still help him do the very best he can. *All* children need to learn as much in school as possible, *regardless of their basic ability.* And remember that one day your child might surprise you and everyone else.

Recommendations

(1) Be aware of your child's unique abilities in various subjects. You don't need the results of long, complex testing by an expert to determine your child's abilities. In most cases, you can find them out simply by talking with your child's teachers and school counselor and seeing how your child does in various subject areas when he works hard. Once you know your child's abilities, you can quickly help him if he has difficulties by concentrating on the troublesome area.

(2) If your child lacks basic ability in a subject, a major key to avoiding problems or failures is to strive to set schoolwork goals geared to his ability. The average or standard for your child's class or grade level might not always be the best gauge for his own ability level or rate of progress. As we noted earlier in this chapter, you can work with your child's teachers to make sure all his schoolwork is challenging but fits his needs. You also can help him learn to set challenging yet achievable goals for himself.

(3) A child who lacks basic ability needs regularly scheduled homework. He needs to spend quiet time really concentrating on schoolwork to learn it and also needs to review repeatedly what he has already learned. Recently, researchers found that low-ability students who did just one to three hours of homework a week usually got grades as high as average-ability students who did not do homework.

(4) Finally, remember that although basic ability certainly influences what a child can learn, it's not nearly as important as his study habits and desire to succeed. When a child wants to learn, tries hard, and has the skills he needs to be a good learner, his basic intellectual capacity plays a much smaller role in his school success.

PLACEMENT IN LOWER ABILITY GROUP

Personally, we don't favor grouping by ability, but it's still the practice at many schools. Some parents get very concerned if their child is placed in a lower ability group. One of their main concerns is usually whether their child will be able to go to college after being placed in a lower ability group. If he receives good grades and takes at least a minimal number of math, English,science, and history courses in high school, he will probably be able to go on to college, although not a highly selective one.

A second question parents often ask is "Should I try to get him into a higher ability group?" If your child receives A's in the lower ability group for several consecutive grading periods, consider talking with his teachers or school counselor to try to move him into a higher ability group. If he receives less than "A" grades in the lower ability group, concentrate on improving his grades by following the suggestions in this book.

Placement in a lower ability group doesn't mean that your child can't go on to be successful in school and life. Remember, many successful people, including Albert Einstein, were considered during their school years to have "low ability."

Conclusion

If your child has learning or behavior problems that interfere with his school success, you can help in a number of ways. The best contribution you can make is to help him learn and practice the basic principles for school success: establishing a regular study schedule, acquiring good study habits and skills, and getting motivated to succeed. Most children can either overcome or compensate for learning or behavior problems with common-sense guidance from teachers, counselors, and parents—if the children understand and practice the basics. Without the basics, no amount of aid from parents, teachers, counselors, or even specialists is likely to help them improve their school performance.

Remember, also, that success leads to success. So when problems occur, you must try even harder to encourage and reward any successes. Success builds confidence and motivation, qualities that children who are having difficulty really need.

Getting Involved in the Schools

One way to help your child succeed is to become involved in the school yourself and establish good communication with the school personnel. You can find out some things by talking with your child and other parents and by reviewing your child's schoolbooks and homework assignments, but to help effectively, you need to know what goes on in the school firsthand. You'll find it easy to get involved.

Getting the Most Out of Parent-Teacher Conferences

Parent-teacher conferences let you get to know your child's teachers and other school personnel and share information about your child with them. They also provide good opportunities to find out about your child's specific program and daily activities.

Most teachers arrange formal parent-teacher conferences several times each year. But don't hesitate to request one at another time—most teachers welcome parental interest and would be happy to meet with you. Just call ahead to arrange a mutually convenient time.

A POINT TO PONDER

It's important that your child's teachers and principal get to know you. If they do, your child will feel safer and the school personnel will notice her more. (Colin Greer, *Parade Magazine*).

You will likely gain a great deal simply by going to parent-teacher conferences, listening to the teacher and other personnel, and sharing your concerns with them. However, you can take a number of steps to make sure that you get the most out of the conferences.

Using Conferences to Help Your Child

Look at parent-teacher conferences as times when you and the teacher can figure out together the best way to help your child succeed in school. It's a time to solve problems and collaborate on strategies to help her.

Developing Questions in Advance

Before you go to the conference, take a few minutes to jot down any questions you might have. Just asking some general questions might yield some interesting, useful information. Some questions you might want to ask include:

- Can you tell me about or show me some of the typical things my child does each day at school?

- What do you expect my child to learn in her various subjects this year?

- What are my child's strong and weak subjects?

- What can I do at home to help my child do better in school?

By asking such questions, you'll probably learn a great deal about your child's school program and her teachers' expectations for her. You'll also pick up some ideas for helping her at home to improve her school performance.

Listing Your Concerns

List any concerns about your child that you would like to share with her teacher—for example, if your child seems to spend inordinate amounts of time on one subject. Express your concerns in a positive, diplomatic way. Before the conference ends, be sure you both focus on how you can work *together* to solve any concerns or problems.

Involving Your Child

Before you attend the conference, ask your child what she would like you to find out from or share with her teacher. Your child spends many hours at school every day and probably has some questions or concerns. Her questions might be as simple as, "How are grades determined in history class?"—something she might feel she should know but doesn't want to ask. You can ask such questions for her and, in the process, add to your knowledge.

If it's appropriate, you might want your child to attend the conference with you. Sometimes you can accomplish a lot when everybody sits down together. Be sure to check with the teacher to see if bringing your child is acceptable. And make sure that your child wants to go—if none of the other children attends, she might feel awkward or embarrassed.

A POINT TO PONDER

Children learn best from someone they respect. So, avoid putting down the teacher in front of your child. Do not say the teacher is "too strict" or "too fussy" or "doesn't know what she is talking about." If you have criticism, take it to the teacher. If that doesn't clear it up, discuss it with the principal. (Claire Safran, *Reader's Digest,* September, 1985).

Developing Working Partnerships with Teachers

At the conference, don't feel intimidated by or act superior to your child's teachers. Teachers are people just like everybody else, with families, jobs, and problems just like yours.

Elevating either the teachers or yourself to a higher level only prevents you from being effective. Approach the conference just as you approach a conversation with anyone else you respect and want to get to know and like.

Listening and Questioning for Understanding

Listen to what the teacher has to say and don't be afraid to ask questions if you don't understand something. If she uses educational jargon or says something you don't understand, ask questions. If you don't understand something, chances are the teacher hasn't explained it clearly. There is nothing you need to know that can't be explained in clear, everyday language.

Being Positive About Your Child

Always accentuate the positive about your child. Ask the teacher to tell you about your child's academic and social successes.

Also, tell the teacher positive things about your child. Don't avoid discussing problems or concerns, but do try to focus on the positive. You want the teacher to have a positive, not a negative, image of your child.

Focusing on Solutions, Not Problems

Take a problem-solving approach. If the teacher starts telling you about academic or discipline problems your child has, listen carefully and ask what each of you can do to solve them. In other words, try to focus on positive things and on solving problems. The least productive kind of conference is one that becomes just a discussion of your child's problems.

Being Friendly and Cooperative

Approach every conference with a friendly, cooperative attitude and try to maintain it throughout the meeting, even if the teacher's attitude seems negative or uncooperative.

In rare cases, you might need to complain or be demanding but, in the vast majority of cases, your child will best benefit if you are calm, positive, and cooperative. If you are friendly and cooperative, almost every teacher will be friendly and cooperative toward you.

Being friendly and cooperative does not mean, however, that you shouldn't ask questions and communicate concerns in a clear, straightforward way. For example, you might ask "How can we get Suzie to spend more time on her reading activities?" rather than "You should make Suzie spend more time on reading activities." This difference is subtle but significant.

A POINT TO PONDER

Remember, the purpose of parent-teacher conferences is to help your child, so let her know what happens. Share with her any goals that you and the teacher develop. Discuss any problems with your child in a positive way, and try to understand her point of view.

Joining the Parent-Teacher Association

A second way to get involved in your child's school is to join the parent-teacher association (PTA). You might only have time to read the organization's newsletters and journals, which often contain ideas on helping your child succeed in school. Or, you might attend regular meetings or even become active in organizing and arranging activities.

By going to PTA meetings, you can get to know both school personnel and other parents. You'll find out what's happening in the school as well as what other parents are doing to help their children succeed.

By staying on top of what's happening you'll be sure that your child receives the best of what the school has to offer. You'll also pick up many ideas about how to help your child succeed from other parents, school personnel, and speakers at PTA meetings.

THE "PERFECT" GIFT

Recently, Sara Evans suggested in *Parents Magazine* that she had found the "perfect" gift for your child's teacher. No, it isn't an apple! Instead, it's a note of encouragement and thanks to the teacher for what she has done for the class and, in particular, for your child. Most notes between parents and teachers concern problems, so a note of encouragement and thanks is a gift that the teacher often treasures. It's more meaningful than a box of stationery, bars of scented soap, or candy. It tells the teacher that she is doing a good job. It also gives you an opportunity to look for the good things going on in your child's school and helps you become more aware of what's meaningful and worthwhile for your child.

More Ways to Get Involved

In addition to making the most of parent-teacher conferences and joining the PTA, you can take other steps to get to know and share information with teachers and other school personnel.

Attending School Activities

Try attending school-sponsored activities regularly (for example, sports events, musical and theatrical events, comedy or variety shows, booster clubs, bazaars, or open houses). These activities provide a chance to get to know school personnel. It doesn't really matter which activities you attend so long as you participate.

Volunteering

If you have the time, try volunteering to supervise field trips or help with special events in your child's classroom. Together with attending school activities, doing volunteer work can help you better understand what's required of your child in school.

Getting Involved in School Governance

You might also want to get involved in school governance. Keeping up with school policies, changes, issues such as funding priorities, and new program development can make you more aware of what's occurring in your child's school and other schools in the district. If you attend school board meetings and help lobby for educational programs, personnel, and equipment by writing your elected representatives, you'll help not only your child but other children as well. If you support your local schools and act as an advocate, you'll better their chances of obtaining the resources they need to help your child.

Conclusion

You can work with school personnel to help your child in a number of ways. Involvement with the school, particularly in parent-teacher conferences, is important for helping your child succeed. Choose a level of involvement you find comfortable, one that fits the time you have available, and focus on things that will help your child.

You need not feel obligated to take part in all or even most of the activities discussed in this chapter. Taking on too much responsibility will detract from helping your child, your family, and yourself at home. So pick things you enjoy and that will best benefit your child and her schoolmates.

Finding Help
When It Is Needed

Despite your best efforts, there will probably be times when your child needs more help than you can offer. Most communities have resources available to help in such situations.

Recognizing When Your Child Needs Help

The first step is to recognize when your child needs or could benefit from outside help. He might need help for a number of reasons.

Do You Have Enough Time to Help?

An increasingly common reason for securing outside help is that many parents just don't have enough time to help. The number of one-parent families is growing, as is the number of families in which both parents work full time outside the home. In either case, the parents face a real dilemma because they often are too busy or too tired to give their child the help he needs with his schoolwork. If you find yourself in this dilemma, don't just feel guilty or overextend yourself, so that you rush or neglect things. Instead, learn how to recognize when your child needs outside support and how to find it.

Is the Subject Matter Unfamiliar to You?

Another time to secure outside assistance arises when your child needs help on a subject with which you are unfamiliar. For instance, he might need help with advanced calculus, computer programming, a foreign language, or some other subject you know little about. At such times it's usually better to find someone well versed in the subject than to try to learn about it quickly yourself.

Are Your Attempts to Help Unsuccessful?

A third reason for getting outside assistance is if your child is having trouble and your assistance doesn't seem to be doing much good. Sometimes, no matter how hard you try, you might be unable to help your child learn a new skill or understand and remember something. For example, you might have difficulty helping your child develop and coordinate all the skills he needs to become a fluent reader who comprehends whatever he reads. Learning to read is a very complex task. Rather than frustrating both yourself and your child, consider getting outside help.

Sources of Assistance

Once you have determined that your child needs outside help, you must then figure out what type of help he needs. You'll find that you have several options.

Tutors

One of the best, most inexpensive ways to get help for your child is to hire a tutor, that is, a person to work with your child one-to-one. A tutor can help when your child has trouble with a particular subject, needs extra guided practice, or just needs help with his homework assignments. Tutors usually work for a reasonable fee and can help your child in a variety of ways.

To be effective, a tutor must know the subject matter, have patience, and be willing to help. Don't expect a tutor to come with a special degree or certification. Tutors can be considered qualified if they have expertise in the subject matter and a personality suited to working with children.

Sometimes you can find professional tutors or teachers seeking part-time work, but many other people in your community are also good candidates. Many senior citizens, for example, are retired teachers or are well versed in a subject and would enjoy tutoring at a minimal cost to you.

Try calling your local retired citizens' association to see who might be available, or simply advertise in the newspaper.

You might also find local high school or college students who can help your child for a minimal sum. An older student who babysits your child after school might also be able to help with his homework. Even an older brother or sister might be willing and able to tutor him.

Before you hire a tutor, make sure he or she is willing to focus on your child's actual schoolwork. Some tutors want to introduce new tasks or information, which requires your child to do his regular schoolwork plus the work the tutor assigns. The last thing your child might need is *more* work—if he needs a tutor, he's probably having enough trouble just completing his regular work. Tutors who use just the regular schoolwork can be very effective (Marty Nemko and Barbara Nemko, *Getting a Private School Education in a Public School,* Acropolis Books, 1986).

A POINT TO PONDER

Because most parents love their children so much, they desperately want them to get a good education. As a result, some parents get easily frustrated and impatient when their child has trouble with a subject. If this happens to you, try to find a tutor to help during your child's study times.

Also, if you and your child tend to argue when you're trying to help him study, we strongly recommend that you hire a tutor. It might make your family life much more calm and pleasant.

Classes

Most communities have evening, summer, or weekend classes that would help your child. Classes might cover subjects such as geometry, reading, or English grammar or school-related skills such as speed reading, using the library, using a home computer, typing, or improving study habits. These classes might help your child learn a difficult subject, provide him with either a refresher or practical experience, or teach him new skills to help him do schoolwork.

Classes that might benefit your child are widely available in most communities. Local schools usually offer summer sessions or courses, and many community colleges and agencies (for example, recreation departments) offer evening or weekend classes. Some community businesses sponsor courses—for example, an electronics store might hold classes on using home computers. And some organizations or private specialists in education conduct workshops or mini-courses.

To find out what courses are offered in your community, contact your local school board office or look for educational opportunities listed in the phone book or advertised in the newspaper.

Specialists

You might also find local specialists on a subject who could assist your child. Your child might require help from a specialist if he is having particular difficulty with a subject and he can't overcome it even with help from you, his teacher, and a tutor. Reading specialists are probably the best known; others include speech therapists and science, mathematics, English, foreign language, and writing specialists.

You can usually find specialists in various subjects through neighborhood schools, community colleges, and universities. They might be teachers, professors, or educational consultants. Graduate students in universities can sometimes offer the expertise you need at a very reasonable cost. You'll also find some educational specialists listed in the phone book. If you can't find a specialist in the field you need, call your local school board office and ask for the address or phone number of a professional organization in that field (for example, the International Reading Association or the Association for Mathematics Teachers). Contact the organization and request a list of members in your area whom you could contact about helping your child.

Psychologists or Counselors

You can also get assistance for your child from psychologists and counselors who have training or experience in school-related problems. They can often provide good advice on many school-related concerns. For example, they can suggest or help set up study schedules and rules. They can also provide advice on getting along with teachers and classmates and on choosing classes or courses of study, schools, and future careers.

You can usually find school psychologists or counselors, like educational specialists, through the schools. You can also find them through colleges or universities, hospitals or other medical facilities, and the phone book. Again, if you can't find one, contact your local school board office and request the address and phone number of a state or national organization for school psychologists or counselors, and then contact the organization for more information.

Conclusion

At various times throughout your child's school years, you might need outside help with his education. Most children need only short-term help, and if they get it at the right times, it can help them tremendously.

Promoting Education in the Home

Research has shown over and over that children's home and family environments have a major impact on their educational achievements. Thus, you want to make sure the environment in your home is conducive to educational success.

We offer a number of ideas for making your family environment educationally stimulating. You'll need to determine which ideas would be easiest and most enjoyable for your family and would best benefit your child. First, consider which activities would fit easily into your family's schedule. Then consider your family members' interests and your child's age and skills.

Organizing Your Home

If you arrange your home carefully, you can help make learning an easier, more natural part of your child's life.

Enjoyable Learning Materials

Try to make items available in your home that stimulate your child's interest in learning and that make learning fun. Subscribe to magazines suitable for her age, interests, and reading ability. If your child gets her own magazines regularly, she'll be more likely to read for enjoyment.

Also try to have books related to your child's interests available at home. In fact, it's best to leave them lying around with other family members' reading materials for your child to pick up and enjoy. You can check out a wide range of books from the public library; then gradually increase the amount of text as your child takes more interest in them. In addition, as noted in Chapter 6, remember that books make good gifts that your child can use to build a permanent library.

PRACTICING READING AND WRITING

The best way for a child to improve her reading and writing skills is simply by practicing them. Writing personal notes is a good way to practice.

Write your child notes and encourage her to write back. You can write notes to pass on information, give directions on how to do something, or simply send a friendly greeting. For example, a note put in a packed lunch might say, "I hope you like your bologna sandwich and chocolate chip cookies. When you get home this afternoon we are going shopping at the mall. You can ask Lisa if she would like to go along. Love, Mom."

The complexity of the notes can increase as your child's skills improve.

Enjoyable Learning Activities

Fun learning activities can become a part of your family's routine. Try posting news clippings or cartoons your child might enjoy on a family bulletin board or the refrigerator. You can use them as topics of conversation.

Another idea is to install a backyard mailbox so your child can share notes and letters with neighborhood friends. This can improve both her reading and writing skills.

Family Quiet Time

Many families schedule a daily quiet time in their homes. Quiet time can give your child a natural opportunity to read, study, and think or to write letters, poems, stories, or ideas. A quiet, relaxed time at home each day can also reduce stress and help your child develop a habit that could improve her chances for reading and learning throughout her life.

The Example of Lifelong Learning

Perhaps most important, set a good example for your child. This cannot be overemphasized. Let your child see you reading and doing quiet study work (for example, balancing the budget, learning how to build or fix something, or studying a map to plan a trip). By setting a good example, you'll show your child in the most effective way possible that learning, reading, and studying are important skills she'll need throughout her life.

Mealtime Activities

In most households, the evening meal is one of the few times when family members can get together and share information about their daily activities. Be sure to take advantage of it.

Ask About the Day's Events

While you are preparing the meal, eating, and cleaning up, encourage your child to talk about school, what she is studying, and new ideas or current events she has learned about. And share with her anything new or interesting you did or learned during the day.

A POINT TO PONDER

Young children are notorious for asking lots of questions. This behavior provides you with an excellent opportunity for encouraging their curiosity about the world. It also gives you a natural time to explain how to find answers by using reference books (for example, dictionaries or encyclopedias) or asking people who might know.

When your child asks questions, be careful you don't discourage her. If you repeatedly discourage her questions, you could affect her intellectual growth. This doesn't mean, however, that you must answer all her questions. Instead, encourage her to find the answers herself. You'll help her build self-direction, independence, and a solid foundation for educational success.

Share New Words

Mealtime is also a good time for vocabulary development. Make an effort to use new words in daily conversation and explain what they mean. Also, encourage word sharing by having family members discuss new or uncommon words they encountered during the day, including what they mean and how to use them.

Be a Positive Listener

Whenever your child is communicating her ideas, don't discourage her by nagging or focusing on mistakes. Feel free to ask questions, encourage appropriate attitudes and behaviors, and, when necessary, correct mistakes, but be sure you're positive and diplomatic. Focusing on your child's mistakes during your conversations could make her hesitant to express new ideas, try new words, or discuss what she is doing in school.

Trips

Family trips, both short and long, provide lots of experiences that can help your child with her schoolwork. They furnish a good opportunity to help your child become an astute observer and share her ideas and experiences with other family members.

Learning from Pleasure Trips

When you're planning a pleasure trip, try to consider events that are beneficial to your child's learning. Family outings to a library, science museum, historical area, or art display can be fun and informative, but so can trips to a county fair, beach, or amusement park. Camping trips or visits with friends or family can be valuable learning experiences as well. Capitalize on a trip to the beach, for example, by having relaxed, fun discussions on the differences between rivers, lakes, and oceans and the various types and sizes of fish, birds, and other animals that live there.

Every new situation offers lots of potential learning experiences. Think about them beforehand so you can help your child learn as well as have fun.

Learning from Road and Commercial Signs

When you take a trip, whether it's long or short, call your child's attention to signs posted along the road. Encourage preschool children to read familiar signs and logos, such as a McDonald's sign or the symbols or words on restroom doors. This helps young children develop their visual memory and their understanding of what reading is all about.

For older children, games such as recognizing license plates from various states or figuring distances from mileage signs can help them practice their reading and math skills and improve their visual discrimination. For adolescents, watching for the makes of cars, identifying which country foreign cars are from, and interpreting road signs can be pleasant ways to spend travel time.

Developing Travel Skills

On long trips, introduce your child to map reading and computing mileage and travel time. Depending on your child's age, share with or even turn over to her the duty of planning the route and acting as a guide. Also get her involved in reading timetables or directions or in guiding the family to the proper ticket counter, gate, or taxi stand.

Include other worthwhile travel experiences on your agenda. Ask your child to read the menu when you're dining out, figure out the best value for the money when you're shopping, and even help fill in forms when you're checking into a motel or commenting on the quality of service.

Trips can provide a wealth of challenging learning experiences for your child. However, make sure that both you and your child remember to just relax and have fun. Learning experiences, whether they're planned or spontaneous, should be as fun and relaxed as possible.

Household Chores

Household chores provide a wide range of opportunities to encourage skills that can lead to school success. In addition, doing daily chores can foster decision-making skills and a sense of responsibility and independence.

Using Simple, Everyday Opportunities

To use chores as learning experiences, take advantage of opportunities that are available everyday. Helpful activities can be as simple as finding a number in a telephone directory, sorting clothes by color for washing, timing food baking in the oven, or reading meters and gauges around the house. You can also foster skills such as problem solving, critical thinking, and using resource materials by having your child tackle more complex activities like balancing a checkbook or making a shopping list. Making a shopping list might seem simple, but it requires figuring out what and how much you need for a given period, reading the newspaper for sale items, learning to spell the items you need, and figuring out how to stay within your budget.

Considering Your Child's Age and Interests

When you involve your child in household chores, be sure to consider her age and interests. If she shows an interest in certain types of projects, try to let her help as much as possible. Children often express an interest in cooking, decorating, or building projects. Use these interests to foster learning.

Using Activities as Supplements to Schoolwork

Although household duties are good learning experiences for your child, they must not be allowed to detract from schoolwork or other learning experiences. For instance, if your child has an opportunity to visit the state capitol or a museum, make a special effort to rearrange her schedule to accommodate this unique learning experience. Likewise, don't let household chores interfere with studying or even recreational reading. In fact, if you want your child to succeed in school, make both studying and recreational reading high priorities in your home.

Free Time

In our society, the main free-time activity for both children and adults is watching television. Unfortunately, too much television can be harmful. Television has been called a "mind drug" for children, because it makes them passive receivers of information, much of which is of questionable value. This doesn't mean, however, that all television viewing is bad. Some programs are very educational and can help your child develop the vocabulary and general knowledge she needs to succeed in school.

Sometimes you can use television to actively promote learning. *T.V. Tips for Parents* is a new twenty-page booklet created by The Corporation for Public Broadcasting. The booklet provides ideas for parents on making television a tool for learning. For example, you and your child can play television word or fact games along with the contestants. To get this free booklet, send a self-addressed, business-size envelope with fifty-six cents in postage to The Corporation for Public Broadcasting, Department P, P.O. Box 33039, Washington, D.C. 20033.

Monitoring the Content of Television Viewing

When you permit your child to watch television, monitor the shows she watches. Encourage her to watch informative, fun programs with positive values, rather than shows with violence and other questionable messages. Depending on your child's age, shows such as the evening news, *National Geographic* specials, and *The Cosby Show* can be both informative and fun.

Restricting the Amount of Television

To succeed in school, your child needs to be an active, thinking member of society—which is not likely to happen if she watches television all the time. Encourage her to think of new ideas, participate in a variety of activities, and evaluate what goes on around her. Make sure she limits her television viewing to a reasonable amount each day.

DEVELOPING A TV SCHEDULE

A recent article in *PTA Today* (March, 1987) suggested that a positive way to regulate the amount and content of your child's TV viewing is to spend some time together reading and discussing the weekly TV listings. You can then cooperate on making a schedule of shows to watch during the week. This activity also helps strengthen reading and communication skills and fosters mutual understanding between you and your child.

Providing Alternatives to Television

Once you restrict television viewing, your child will have more free time to do other things. She can use this free time to do things that are fun and at the same time have educational value.

(1) Help your child start a collection of something—perhaps shells, stamps, baseball cards, rocks, or pictures of animals. She should choose something that interests her and that she can label, put into categories, and study. Working on a collection will help develop her discrimination and thinking skills.

(2) Collect forms and applications wherever you find them. These forms might include employment applications, income tax returns, drivers license applications, or credit applications. As soon as your child is old enough, she can practice filling them in and use them in fantasy play. Even young children can partially fill in the forms. This activity will help your child's reasoning, writing, and spelling skills.

READING RESOURCE BOOKS FOR RECREATION

If your preschool child asks you to read her a story during her free time, take advantage of the opportunity. Reading from a children's encyclopedia or books about famous people or different places or books about problem solving can introduce your child to a wealth of worthwhile information in a natural, enjoyable way.

An older child can read such books herself. However, you might have to provide encouragement to get her started.

---

(3) An older child can read stories and articles from magazines, newspapers, or books into a tape recorder so that hospitalized people, elderly friends or relatives, or visually impaired people can listen to them. This will enable her to help others while improving her reading skills.

(4) Encourage your child to share stories with other family members. Parents are always instructed to read to their children, yet all family members, including children, can benefit from reading to others and sharing what they learn. Set aside several times a week for family members to share something they have read. Even a preschool child can participate by showing and explaining pictures in a story or book. Your child will not only practice her reading, thinking, and communication skills, but will also learn the roles of reading and discussion in communication.

CLASSIC COMICS AS RECREATIONAL READING

Many children enjoy reading comic books. If your child likes comics, you might want to purchase comic books that present classic or historical plays and literature. These can be enjoyable, very worthwhile free-time reading.

---

(5) Encourage your child to spend time playing. Choose toys and games that encourage her to be active and creative. Word games such as "Scrabble" can help build her vocabulary. Many other toys and games on the market also build math and reasoning skills. Ask your child's teacher or a toy-store manager to suggest toys geared to your child's age. By selecting games and toys with care, you'll help your child have fun and at the same time learn valuable skills she needs for school success.

(6) Give your child a newspaper page and have her circle a certain letter or word everywhere it occurs. As she gets older and her reading skills improve, have her identify the main ideas or characters in each article.

(7) Encourage your child to write a book on a topic that interests her and others, and then give it to someone as a gift. Such a book could include almost anything—stories, photographs, poems, or recipes for favorite foods. A book describing family or neighborhood activities could be not only a fun learning project for your child, but also a much-appreciated gift for a relative who lives far away or a friend who has moved away.

A POINT TO PONDER

Encourage children who have not yet developed writing skills to tell stories and relate events by drawing pictures. They can use this technique to make books for others, while learning skills like picking a theme, developing a topic, and organizing and putting things in sequential order.

ENCOURAGING CONSTRUCTIVE USE OF FREE TIME

When you encourage your child to use her free time constructively, try to "catch" her doing something worthwhile and let her know it pleased you. For example, smile or tell her that you're pleased to see her reading for enjoyment or watching a documentary on TV.

If she does something you don't like (for example, spending too much time watching TV, talking on the phone, or playing video games), remember that you can't change everything at once. Try to change only one behavior at a time and focus your attention on praising any desirable things she does during free time.

In summary, constructive use of free time can give your child many learning experiences that will help her in school. You'll need to supply active interest, involvement, direction, and a watchful eye, particularly at first, to help get her oriented toward using her free time productively. There will and *should* be times when you and your child do things simply for fun and relaxation, regardless of their educational value, but many activities can be fun and relaxing and have educational value as well.

Conclusion

An educationally stimulating home environment and a supportive family can help your child succeed in school. In this chapter, we have outlined a number of suggestions for creating a home setting that will foster your child's educational success. Make sure you consider your family's habits, traditions, and activities, and then select suggestions your family will feel comfortable with, so you can develop an educationally stimulating home environment.

APPENDIX A

Skills for School Success Diagnostic Checklist
(PARENT'S FORM)

GENERAL DIRECTIONS: We recommend that you read chapters one through six before completing this checklist.

The checklist is divided into five general sections (for example, organization, motivation). Within each section, put a check mark by each skill that your child demonstrates consistently. The more unchecked skills there are in a section, the more it needs attention. As your child becomes more proficient, you can check off more items. Once every item is checked off, you'll know your child has the basic skills needed to succeed in school. Try to involve your child in completing the checklist. That is, discuss with your child what should and should not be checked off and why.

If you are in doubt about a skill, review the information about that skill in the book to help you determine whether your child demonstrates it. Consult the checklist to find the page numbers where information appears in the book. Also, after you read the book in a general way, try rereading and concentrating on those parts that deal with the unchecked skills on the checklist.

Finally, we recommend using this checklist every few weeks to a month, to reevaluate your child's skills to see whether he or she is making progress.

Student's Name: _____

Date: _____

Specific Instructions: After reading chapters one through six, put a check mark next to those skills your child demonstrates. Check only those items you are certain your child demonstrates consistently.

Organization (pages 4–9)

_____ Maintains a regular study schedule. (pages 4–7)

_____ Has a quiet, organized place to study. (pages 7–9)

_____ Studies when most alert. (pages 8–9)

_____ Does not let distractions (for example, phone calls) interfere with study. (pages 7–8)

_____ Gathers all needed books and tools in the study area before study time begins. (pages 5–6)

Study Skills (pages 10–28)

_____ Reads and understands homework assignments. (pages 10–15)

_____ Understands how to prepare for tests. (pages 15–20)

_____ Finds and uses resource materials. (pages 20–23)

_____ Organizes and develops assigned school papers. (pages 23–27)

Motivation (pages 29–42)

_____ Develops daily study goals. (pages 29–31)

_____ Wants to learn and succeed in school. (pages 31–37)

_____ Respects education. (pages 37–39)

_____ Is independent and self-directed in carrying out school assignments. (pages 39–42)

Stress (pages 43–58)

_____ Able to reduce or prevent unnecessary school-related stress. (pages 47–51)

_____ Can cope with necessary school-related stress. (pages 51–58)

Other Learning and Behavior Skills (pages 59–82)

_____ Sticks to a school task until completed. (pages 59–61)

_____ Remembers what needs to be done and material studied. (pages 61–64)

_____ Uses reading and spelling skills in the process of studying and learning. (pages 64–68)

_____ Cooperates with parents in planning and carrying out school assignments. (pages 69–72)

_____ Likes school and school activities. (pages 74–76)

_____ Is confident and has good self-concept in regard to schoolwork. (pages 76–78)

_____ Pays close attention when doing schoolwork. (pages 78–80)

_____ Understands abilities and talents and capitalizes on them in school. (pages 80–82)

APPENDIX B

Skills for School Success Diagnostic Checklist
(TEACHER'S FORM)

GENERAL DIRECTIONS: The checklist is divided into five sections (for example, organization, motivation). Within each section, put a check mark by each skill that the student demonstrates consistently, that is, every school day. The more unchecked skills listed for each section, the greater the need for attention. As the student becomes more proficient, you can check off more items. Once every item is checked off, you'll know the student has the basic skills needed to succeed in school. If time permits, try to involve the student in completing the checklist. That is, discuss with the child what should and should not be checked and why.

You can look at the page numbers on the checklist to see where information about each skill appears in the book. If you are in doubt about a skill, it may be useful to review the information about that skill in the book, to help you more easily evaluate whether the student demonstrates it.

After completing the checklist, share the results with the student's parents so they'll know in which specific areas they can help their child at home. Consult the page numbers on the checklist to find out where specific skills are discussed in the book, so you can give the parents suggestions for helping their child. You might also want to refer the parents to the book itself, so they can read in detail what they can do to help.

Student's Name: _____

Date: _____

Specific Directions: Put a checkmark next to those skills the student demonstrates in school. Check only those items you are certain the student demonstrates consistently.

Organization (pages 4–9)

_____ Brings completed homework assignments to class. (page 6)

_____ Is prepared for class discussion and other classroom activities. (pages 5–6)

Study Skills (pages 10–28)

_____ Reads and understands school assignments. (pages 10–15)

_____ Performs well on tests in school. (pages 15–20)

_____ Finds and uses resource materials. (pages 20–23)

_____ Organizes and develops assigned school papers. (pages 23–27)

Motivation (pages 29–42)

_____ Carries out tasks assigned by the teacher. (pages 29–31)

_____ Works hard to complete schoolwork correctly. (pages 29–31)

_____ Wants to learn and appears proud of what is learned. (pages 31–33)

_____ Is independent and self-directed in carrying out school assignments. (pages 39–42)

Stress (pages 43–58)

_____ Able to reduce or prevent unnecessary school-related stress. (pages 47–51)

_____ Can cope with necessary school-related stress. (pages 51–58)

Other Learning and Behavior Skills (pages 59–82)

_____ Sticks to a school task until completed. (pages 59–61)

_____ Remembers what needs to be done and material studied. (pages 61–64)

_____ Uses reading and spelling skills in the process of studying and learning. (pages 64–68)

_____ Cooperates with the teacher(s) in planning and carrying out school assignments. (pages 69–72)

_____ Likes school and school activities. (pages 74–76)

_____ Is confident and has good self-concept in regard to schoolwork. (pages 76–78)

_____ Pays close attention when doing schoolwork. (pages 78–80)

_____ Understands abilities and talents and capitalizes on them in school. (pages 80–82)

Free Stuff For Kids—12th Edition

by The Free Stuff Editors
Over 250 free and up-to-two-dollar
educational and fun things kids can send
for by mail. This classic children's activity
book teaches kids the basics of letter
writing. It's a learning tool in disguise. Over
one million copies sold.
$3.95
Ordering #: 2190

Wordplay

by Charles Thiesen and Deanna King
An alternative to run-of-the-mill activity
books that stimulates kids 8-14 to think
and write creatively by solving secret
codes, making up wild stories, writing
funny ads, inventing tongue-twisters and
more. Wordplay is so much fun, kids
don't realize they're learning.
$5.95
Ordering #: 2200

Discipline Without Shouting or Spanking

*by Jerry Wyckoff, Ph.D.,
and Barbara C. Unell*
Helps parents solve the most common
preschool behavior problems; tells how
to discipline in a loving yet firm way.
$4.95
Ordering #: 1079

Webster's Dictionary Game

by Wilbur Webster
Dictionary game fans will love this wacky
word game invented by the black sheep
of the famous dictionary family. Includes
a special dictionary of over 5,000 esoteric
words.
$5.95
Ordering #: 6030

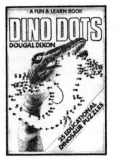

Dino Dots

by Dougal Dixon
This fascinating connect-the-dots puzzle
book features 25 prehistoric wonders.
Each page presents a "name this dinosaur" quiz with lots of numbered dots
to connect. Included are facts about each
dinosaur, which makes this a learn-as-
you-play book.
$4.95
Ordering #: 2250

How to Survive High School
with Minimal Brain Damage

by Doug Lansky and Aaron Dorfman
This hilarious guide tells students how to
be cool in high school. It contains hun-
dreds of pranks, hoaxes and dirty tricks.
"The greatest invention for high school
kids since Cliffs Notes."—Dave Barry.
$4.95
Ordering #: 4050

A,B,C... Play with me!

by Roger Paré
A Read & Play Learning Set
This exciting way to learn the alphabet includes a delightfully illustrated book, amusing games, entertaining puzzles and a teaching guide all in one package.

The book is colorful and clever. The games show children how to play word scrambles, crosswords and anagrams. The puzzles teach observation and motor skills. This set won Roger Paré the award for Canadian Children's Illustrator of the Year.
$12.95

Ordering #: 2230

1,2,3... Play with me!

by Roger Paré
A Read & Play Learning Set
This exciting way to learn numbers includes a delightfully illustrated book by award-winning Canadian illustrator Roger Paré, four amusing games, 10 entertaining mini-puzzles and a teaching guide all in one package.

The book is colorful and clever. The games show children how to arrange numbers in order, add, subtract and understand the "greater" and "lesser" symbols. The puzzle pairs match numbers with the same quantities of objects.
$12.95

Ordering #: 2240

The stork didn't bring me.

by Marie-Francine Hébert
Illustrations by Darcia Labrosse
A Read & Play Learning Set
Teaching young children the birds and bees used to be a fact of life parents faced with fear—until the arrival of this innovative Read & Play Learning Set.

The book is entertaining, colorful and candid. The board game shows how a baby grows in the first nine months after conception. Players roll a die and move their tokens from one month to the next. The guide for parents has all the facts plus suggestions on explaining them to children. What a delightful way to help your child understand where babies come from.
$12.95

Ordering #: 2220

ORDER FORM

Qty.	Order #	Book Title	Author	Price
_____	1210	10,000 Baby Names	Lansky, B.	$2.95
_____	2240	1,2,3 ... Play with me!	Paré, R.	$12.95
_____	2230	A,B,C ... Play with me!	Paré, R.	$12.95
_____	1159	Baby & Child Medical Care	Hart, T.	$5.95
_____	1029	Best Baby Name Book	Lansky, B.	$3.95
_____	1239	Best Baby Shower Book	Cooke, C.	$3.95
_____	1309	Birth Partner's Handbook	Jones, C.	$5.95
_____	1049	David, We're Pregnant!	Johnston, L.	$3.95
_____	1059	Dear Babysitter	Lansky, V.	$8.95
_____	2250	Dino Dots	Dixon, D.	$4.95
_____	1079	Discipline w/o Shouting	Wyckoff, J.	$4.95
_____	4039	Don't Call Mommy at Work	McBride, M.	$4.95
_____	1089	Do They Ever Grow Up?	Johnston, L.	$3.95
_____	1099	Exercises for Baby & Me	Regnier, S.	$9.95
_____	1109	Feed Me! I'm Yours	Lansky, V.	$6.95
_____	1119	First Year Baby Care	Kelly, P.	$5.95
_____	2190	Free Stuff for Kids	FSK Editors	$3.95
_____	4009	Grandma Knows Best	McBride, M.	$4.95
_____	3109	Grandma's Favorites Bragbook	Meadowbrook	$6.50
_____	1139	Hi Mom! Hi Dad!	Johnston, L.	$3.95
_____	4050	How to Survive High School	Lansky/Dorfman	$4.95
_____	1289	Letters from Pregnant Coward	Armor, J.	$6.95
_____	1149	Mother Murphy's Law	Lansky, B.	$2.95
_____	4010	Mother Murphy's 2nd Law	Lansky, B.	$2.95
_____	3249	Mother's Memories	Meadowbrook	$5.95
_____	1179	Practical Parenting Tips	Lansky, V.	$6.95
_____	1189	Self Esteem .. Tots to Teens	Anderson, G.	$5.95
_____	2220	Stork didn't bring me	Hébert, M.	$12.95
_____	1199	Successful Breastfeeding	Dana, Price	$8.95
_____	1330	Visualizations—Easier Chbth	Jones, C.	$4.95
_____	6030	Webster's Dict. Game	Webster, W.	$5.95
_____	3230	While We're Out	Meadowbrook	$3.50
_____	2200	Wordplay	Thiesen, C.	$5.95
_____	1259	Working Woman's Guide to BF	Dana/Price	$5.95

Please send me copies of the books checked above. I am enclosing $_____ which covers the full amount per book shown above plus $1.25 for postage and handling for the first book and $.50 for each additional book. (Add $1.75 postage and handling for each Read & Play Learning Set.) Add $2.00 to total for postage and handling for books shipped to Canada. Overseas postage and handling will be billed. MN residents add 6% sales tax. Allow up to four weeks for delivery. **Quantity discounts available upon request.** Send check or money order to Meadowbrook, Inc. No cash or C.O.D's please.

For purchases over $10.00 you may use VISA or MasterCard (order by mail or phone). For these orders we need the information below.

Charge to: ☐ VISA   ☐ MasterCard Account #_____

Expiration Date_____

Card Signature_____

Send Book(s) to:

Name_____

Address_____

City_____ State_____ Zip_____

Mail order to: Book Orders, Meadowbrook, Inc., 18318 Minnetonka Blvd., Deephaven, MN 55391. Phone orders: Toll Free (800) 338-2232.